Praise for Johnny Townsend

In *Zombies for Jesus*, "Townsend isn't writing satire, but deeply emotional and revealing portraits of people who are, with a few exceptions, quite lovable."

Kel Munger, *Sacramento News and Review*

Townsend's stories are "a gay *Portnoy's Complaint* of Mormonism. Salacious, sweet, sad, insightful, insulting, religiously ethnic, quirky-faithful, and funny."

D. Michael Quinn, author of *The Mormon Hierarchy: Origins of Power*

Johnny Townsend is "an important voice in the Mormon community."

Stephen Carter, editor of *Sunstone* magazine

The Circumcision of God "asks questions that are not often asked out loud in Mormonism, and certainly not answered."

Jeff Laver, author of *Elder Petersen's Mission Memories*

1

"Told from a believably conversational first-person perspective, [*The Abominable Gayman*'s] novelistic focus on Anderson's journey to thoughtful self-acceptance allows for greater character development than often seen in short stories, which makes this well-paced work rich and satisfying, and one of Townsend's strongest. An extremely important contribution to the field of Mormon fiction." Named to Kirkus Reviews' Best of 2011.

Kirkus Reviews

"The thirteen stories in *Mormon Underwear* capture this struggle [between Mormonism and homosexuality] with humor, sadness, insight, and sometimes shocking details....*Mormon Underwear* provides compelling stories, literally from the inside-out."

Niki D'Andrea, *Phoenix New Times*

In *Sex among the Saints,* "Townsend writes with a deadpan wit and a supple, realistic prose that's full of psychological empathy....he takes his protagonists' moral struggles seriously and invests them with real emotional resonance."

Kirkus Reviews

"The Buzzard Tree," from *The Circumcision of God*, was a finalist for the 2007 Whitney Award for Best Short LDS Fiction.

"Townsend's lively writing style and engaging characters [in *Zombies for Jesus*] make for stories which force us to wake up, smell the (prohibited) coffee, and review our attitudes with regard to reading dogma so doggedly. These are tales which revel in the individual tics and quirks which make us human, Mormon or not, gay or not…"

A.J. Kirby, The Short Review

"The Rift," from *The Abominable Gayman*, is a "fascinating tale of an untenable situation…a *tour de force*."

David Lenson, editor, *The Massachusetts Review*

"Pronouncing the Apostrophe," from *The Golem of Rabbi Loew*, is "quiet and revealing, an intriguing tale…"

Sima Rabinowitz, Literary Magazine Review, NewPages.com

The Circumcision of God is "a collection of short stories that consider the imperfect, silenced majority of Mormons, who may in fact be [the Church's] best hope….[The book leaves] readers regretting the church's willingness to marginalize those who best exemplify its ideals: those who love fiercely despite all obstacles, who brave challenges at great personal risk and who always choose the hard, higher road."

Kirkus Reviews

"Johnny Townsend's short stories cannot be pigeon-holed. His keen observations on the human condition come in many shapes and sizes...reflecting on both his Jewish and Mormon backgrounds as well as life in the vast and varied American gay community. He dares to think and write about people and incidents that frighten away more timid artists. His perspective is sometimes startling, sometimes hilarious, sometimes poignant, but always compassionate."

Gerald S. Argetsinger, Artistic Director of the
Hill Cumorah Pageant (1990-96)

In *Mormon Fairy Tales*, Johnny Townsend displays "both a wicked sense of irony and a deep well of compassion."

Kel Munger, *Sacramento News and Review*

"*Selling the City of Enoch* exists at that awkward intersection where the LDS ideal meets the real world, and Townsend navigates his terrain with humor, insight, and pathos."

Donna Banta, author of *False Prophet*

The Golem of Rabbi Loew will prompt "gasps of outrage from conservative readers...a strong collection."

Kirkus Reviews

"That's one of the reasons why I found Johnny Townsend's new book *Mormon Fairy Tales* SO MUCH FUN!! Without fretting about what the theology is supposed to be if it were pinned down, Townsend takes you on a voyage to explore the rich-but-undertapped imagination of Mormonism. I loved his portrait of spirit prison! He really nailed it—not in an official doctrine sort of way, but in a sort of 'if you know Mormonism, you know this is what it must be like' way—and what a prison it is!

Johnny Townsend has written at least ten books of Mormon stories. So far, I've read only two (*Mormon Fairy Tales* and *The Circumcision of God*), but I'm planning to read the rest—and you should too, if you'd like a fun and interesting new perspective on Mormons in life and imagination!"

C. L. Hanson, *Main Street Plaza*

Zombies for Jesus is "eerie, erotic, and magical."

Publishers Weekly

"While [Townsend's] many touching vignettes draw deeply from Mormon mythology, history, spirituality and culture, [*Mormon Fairy Tales*] is neither a gaudy act of proselytism nor angry protest literature from an ex-believer. Like all good fiction, his stories are simply about the joys, the hopes and the sorrows of people."

Kirkus Reviews

"In *Let the Faggots Burn* author Johnny Townsend restores this tragic event [the UpStairs Lounge fire] to its proper place in LGBT history and reminds us that the victims of the blaze were not just 'statistics,' but real people with real lives, families, and friends."

Jesse Monteagudo, The Bilerico Project

Let the Faggots Burn: The UpStairs Lounge Fire is "a gripping account of all the horrors that transpired that night, as well as a respectful remembrance of the victims."

Terry Firma, Patheos

In *Let the Faggots Burn*, "Townsend's heart-rending descriptions of the victims…seem to [make them] come alive once more."

Kit Van Cleave, *OutSmart Magazine*

Marginal Mormons is "an irreverent, honest look at life outside the mainstream Mormon Church….Throughout his musings on sin and forgiveness, Townsend beautifully demonstrates his characters' internal, perhaps irreconcilable struggles….Rather than anger and disdain, he offers an honest portrayal of people searching for meaning and community in their lives, regardless of their life choices or secrets." Named to Kirkus Reviews' Best of 2012.

Kirkus Reviews

"The Sneakover Prince" from *God's Gargoyles* is "one of the most sweet and romantic stor[ies] I have ever read."

Elisa Rolle, Reviews and Ramblings,
founder of The Rainbow Awards

"*Let the Faggots Burn* is a one-of-a-kind piece of history. Without Townsend's diligence and devotion, many details would've been lost forever. With his tremendous foresight and tenacious research, Townsend put a face on this tragedy at a time when few people would talk about it....Through Townsend's vivid writing, you will sense what it must've been like in those final moments as the fire ripped through the UpStairs Lounge. *Let the Faggots Burn* is a chilling and insightful glimpse into a largely forgotten and ignored chapter of LGBT history."

Robert Camina, writer and producer of the
documentary *Raid of the Rainbow Lounge*

"Johnny Townsend's 'Partying with St. Roch' [in the anthology *Latter-Gay Saints*] tells a beautiful, haunting tale."

Kent Brintnall, Out in Print: Queer Book Reviews

Gayrabian Nights is "an allegorical tour de force...a hard-core emotional punch."

Gay. Guy. Reading and Friends

The stories in *The Mormon Victorian Society* "register the new openness and confidence of gay life in the age of same-sex marriage....What hasn't changed is Townsend's wry, conversational prose, his subtle evocations of character and social dynamics, and his deadpan humor. His warm empathy still glows in this intimate yet clear-eyed engagement with Mormon theology and folkways. Funny, shrewd and finely wrought dissections of the awkward contradictions—and surprising harmonies—between conscience and desire." Named to Kirkus Reviews' Best of 2013.

Kirkus Reviews

"This collection of short stories [*The Mormon Victorian Society*] featuring gay Mormon characters slammed [me] in the face from the first page, wrestled my heart and mind to the floor, and left me panting and wanting more by the end. Johnny Townsend has created so many memorable characters in such few pages. I went weeks thinking about this book. It truly touched me."

Tom Webb, judge for The Rainbow Awards
(A Bear on Books)

"The struggles and solutions of the individuals [in *Latter-Gay Saints*] will resonate across faith traditions and help readers better understand the cost of excluding gay members from full religious participation."

Publishers Weekly

Dragons of the Book of Mormon is an "entertaining collection....Townsend's prose is sharp, clear, and easy to read, and his characters are well rendered..."

Publishers Weekly

"The pre-eminent documenter of alternative Mormon lifestyles...Townsend has a deep understanding of his characters, and his limpid prose, dry humor and well-grounded (occasionally magical) realism make their spiritual conundrums both compelling and entertaining. [*Dragons of the Book of Mormon* is] [a]nother of Townsend's critical but affectionate and absorbing tours of Mormon discontent." Named to Kirkus Reviews' Best of 2014.

Kirkus Reviews

"Mormon Movie Marathon," from *Selling the City of Enoch*, "is funny, constructively critical, but also sad because the desire...for belonging is so palpable."

Levi S. Peterson, author of *The Backslider*
and *The Canyons of Grace*

In *Gayrabian Nights*, "Townsend's prose is always limpid and evocative, and...he finds real drama and emotional depth in the most ordinary of lives."

Kirkus Reviews

Selling the City of Enoch is "sharply intelligent...pleasingly complex...The stories are full of...doubters, but there's no vindictiveness in these pages; the characters continuously poke holes in Mormonism's more extravagant absurdities, but they take very little pleasure in doing so....Many of Townsend's stories...have a provocative edge to them, but this [book] displays a great deal of insight as well...a playful, biting and surprisingly warm collection."

Kirkus Reviews

"Among the most captivating of the prose [in *Off the Rocks*, in a piece reprinted from the collection *A Day at the Temple*] was a story by Johnny Townsend illustrating two Mormon missionaries who break the rules of their teachings to spend more time with one another."

Lauren Childers, *Windy City Times*

Gayrabian Nights is a "complex revelation of how seriously soul damaging the denial of the true self can be."

Ryan Rhodes, author of *Free Electricity*

Gayrabian Nights "was easily the most original book I've read all year. Funny, touching, topical, and thoroughly enjoyable."

Rainbow Awards

Lying for the Lord is "one of the most gripping books that I've picked up for quite a while. I love the author's writing style, alternately cynical, humorous, biting, scathing, poignant, and touching.... This is the third book of his that I've read, and all are equally engaging. These are stories that need to be told, and the author does it in just the right way."

Heidi Alsop, Ex-Mormon Foundation Board Member

"If you like short stories and you're interested in the lives of Mormons, you should be following the work of Johnny Townsend. Since he writes from an ex-Mormon perspective, believers often dismiss Townsend's work as biased—or as *a priori* 'an attack on the church'—but I think that's a mistake. Johnny Townsend writes his characters with a great deal of compassion and empathy, whether they're in the church or not...or somewhere in between."

C. L. Hanson, *Main Street Plaza*

"Townsend is a wonderful writer with a wry but sympathetic eye for humans' frailties, and the ways in which religious belief both exacerbate and console them. [*Despots of Deseret* contains] more vibrant parables about doubts and blasphemies that hide beneath a veneer of piety." Named to Kirkus Reviews' Best of 2015.

Kirkus Reviews

In *Lying for the Lord*, Townsend "gets under the skin of his characters to reveal their complexity and conflicts....shrewd, evocative [and] wryly humorous."

Kirkus Reviews

In *Missionaries Make the Best Companions*, "the author treats the clash between religious dogma and liberal humanism with vivid realism, sly humor, and subtle feeling as his characters try to figure out their true missions in life. Another of Townsend's rich dissections of Mormon failures and uncertainties..." Named to Kirkus Reviews' Best of 2015.

Kirkus Reviews

In *Invasion of the Spirit Snatchers*, "Townsend, a confident and practiced storyteller, skewers the hypocrisies and eccentricities of his characters with precision and affection. The outlandish framing narrative is the most consistent source of shock and humor, but the stories do much to ground the reader in the world—or former world—of the characters....A funny, charming tale about a group of Mormons facing the end of the world."

Kirkus Reviews

Townsend's "works are on a cutting edge of history."

Walter Jones, Assistant Head of Special Collections, Marriott Library

The Washing of Brains has "A lovely writing style, and each story was full of unique, engaging characters....immensely entertaining."

Rainbow Awards

"Townsend's collection [*The Washing of Brains*] once again displays his limpid, naturalistic prose, skillful narrative chops, and his subtle insights into psychology...Well-crafted dispatches on the clash between religion and self-fulfillment..."

Kirkus Reviews

The Last Days Linger was awarded Second Place for Best Gay Contemporary General Fiction in the 2017 Rainbow Awards

"While the author is generally at his best when working as a satirist, there are some fine, understated touches in these tales [*The Last Days Linger*] that will likely affect readers in subtle ways....readers should come away impressed by the deep empathy he shows for all his characters—even the homophobic ones."

Kirkus Reviews

Breaking the Promise of the Promised Land

How Religious Conservatives

Failed America

Johnny Townsend

BookLocker

Saint Petersburg, Florida

Published by BookLocker.com, Inc., St. Petersburg, Florida, U.S.A.

BookLocker.com, Inc.

2019

First Edition

Cover design by Todd Engel

Dedicated to

Greta Thunberg

Keinon Carter

Nakabuye Hilda Flavia

Emma González

David Hogg

Malala Yousafzai

Jasilyn Charger

Payal Jangid

the members of Pussy Riot

and all other activists young and old working to make the world a better place

Special thanks to Donna Banta

for her editorial assistance

For some of Donna's own work, check out *Mormon Erotica* and *False Prophet*.

Contents

Introduction: A War on Religion

(published in *Main Street Plaza* on 22 July 2019)

Religious conservatives often accuse secular or inclusive people of conducting a "War on Christmas!" or "War on Religion!" or "War on God!" I would rephrase that. I and many others are anxiously engaged in conducting a war against ignorance, a war against bigotry and selfishness and greed and short-sightedness, a war against oppression and cruelty. I've certainly never protested altruism and compassion and love. If religious conservatives feel threatened by the sins I do address, hiding behind the name of God is like hiding inside a Trojan horse.

"Onward, Christian Soldiers" certainly takes on a different meaning in that light.

I admit that religious conservatives and I see the same actions quite differently, and this is unfortunately the biggest part of the problem. As a Mormon missionary working to convert apostate Catholics in Rome, I was taught (and therefore believed) I was "helping" people.

It wasn't until I returned home and learned about Baptist missionaries trying to convert unsaved Mormons in Salt Lake that I began to understand the concept of cultural imperialism and different points of view. I resisted my heathen professors at the University of New Orleans as they tried to pry my mind open with their liberal, decadent ideas. But—"Danger! Danger, Will Robinson!"—some of those ideas did eventually seep in.

Why did I care if someone chose not to have children? The species was hardly at risk of disappearing through lack of reproduction.

Why did I care if someone chose not to marry?

Why did I care if someone preferred watching a movie over going to church? If they liked tea or coffee? If they wanted a tattoo?

What did I care if someone chose a different course of study, a different style of clothes, a different career, a different life?

The more I thought about it, the more diversity of thought and action I did want.

If Mormons could moan, "What would happen if *everyone* were gay?" I could just as easily ask, "What would happen if *everyone* sold insurance? What would happen if *everyone* became an apostle?"

Society could not function with that kind of homogeneity.

Even as a die-hard, faithful Mormon, I spoke up for gays. If they were sinning, they had every right to do so. When a friend in Elders' Quorum said he thought gays should be put in prison for sodomy, I asked, "And what do you think they'll do there?"

Even as a dedicated Sabbath-day observer, I thought it wrong to enact "blue laws" that forbid businesses to remain open on Sunday. That meant Jews couldn't do any shopping on

Saturday, their Sabbath, and were also denied the opportunity to shop on my Sabbath. Same for Seventh-Day Adventist Christians.

Even as a believing, active Latter-day Saint, I assured a young woman in the Single Adults group that her decision to pursue medical school and marry a man who preferred to stay home and take care of their children was a perfectly good decision and not to let priesthood leaders tell her otherwise. As if she needed me or any other man to validate this or any other decision in the first place.

Once I left the Church in my mid-twenties, my views shifted dramatically, and my former "open-mindedness" proved insufficient to the task of battling oppression in all its cultural, physical, financial, and religious forms.

When my ex-Mormon husband became a Trotsky socialist, I resisted many of the ideas he brought home. I still do.

But one thing is clear—*some* form of socialism is necessary not only for relieving the oppression waged against billions of humans but also for preserving life itself as we face the ultimate global battle for survival.

As a missionary, I learned to take good wherever I found it. Some aspects of Neapolitan culture were good and some bad. Some aspects of Roman culture were good and some bad. When adding the good I found in Italy to the good I found in New Orleans culture, in rural Mississippi culture, in Mormon culture, in gay culture, I surrounded myself with the best set of ethics I could.

I find some good in Jesuit culture, in the culture of Reform Judaism, in Buddhism, in liberation theology, in the Unitarian philosophy, and elsewhere in religious traditions from around the world.

But when religious conservatives leave our "salvation" to an invisible god, they not only give up their own obligation to act but also impede others from acting as well. They are, in effect, conducting a "War on Humanity," a "War on Climate," a "War on Life Itself." When they continue to promote behaviors resulting in an accelerated progression of the current mass extinction event, they have chosen a position I can't ignore.

Yes, this is war, a devastating civil war, where we end up fighting lifelong friends and beloved aunts and nephews, our favorite bishops, sometimes even employers and leaders of our own political parties.

But it's essential that those of us fighting oppression and exploitation prevail. Let's not shy away from labels like "Liberal!" "Socialist!" "Godless!" or anything else religious conservatives might throw at us. We cannot abdicate our duty, our responsibility, and our opportunity.

The Book of Mormon tells us that starting a war is never justified. So let's remember—we didn't start this war. Religious conservatives did.

In the Mishnah, Rabbi Tarfon tells us that, "It is not [our] responsibility to finish the work of perfecting the world, but [we] are not free to desist from it either." But the stakes are higher now than perhaps ever before in the history of our species. We cannot accept slow, incremental change. If the side of reason and compassion doesn't prevail, both sides of this religious war will lose.

Grab What We Can and Run

Addressing the climate emergency means losing much of the life and culture we love.

On Friday, August 26, 2005, I went to a local performance of *Hair* in Uptown New Orleans. The cast did a fine job, and I had a pleasant evening with a good friend.

The next morning, Paul called me. "Are you evacuating?"

"Huh?"

"There's a major hurricane in the Gulf. I'm going to my sister's house in Baton Rouge. Are you going to stay with your family?"

The last time I'd evacuated, my partner Tom and I had been trapped on a congested highway for many hours, inching painfully along in sweltering heat. We watched as someone from the car ahead of us jumped out, ran to a nearby Dairy Queen, and came back with food for her family before the car had even moved ahead twenty feet.

"I don't know," I said. "I'm so tired." Tom had died three months earlier of liver cancer. I'd spent the time since distributing his belongings, straightening out his affairs, and moving into an apartment, all while not losing any hours at work, since I'd used up my leave during Tom's illness. I'd made sure my new place had washer/dryer hookups before signing the lease, but only after I moved in did I realize the laundry doorway was smaller than normal. The appliances Tom and I had didn't fit, and smaller ones were outrageously expensive. But the new machines were in, I was settling down, and I just wanted a weekend to relax.

"Johnny," he said, "it's a category 5."

I turned on the news. While threatening storms often veered away at the last minute, I decided I had better leave, just to be safe. I grabbed a suitcase, threw in a week's worth of meds, my journal, and a couple of changes of clothes. Before I zipped the lid shut, I evaluated the situation once more. Then I shrugged and threw in my passport, my birth certificate, and my resumé. I grabbed Tom's ashes. Then I climbed into my car and drove off.

Several hours later, I arrived at my aunt's house in Hammond, sixty miles away.

I never saw my apartment again.

When the electricity finally came back on at my aunt's house, I jumped on the computer and bought a plane ticket to Seattle. Tom had loved our visits to the city, and since I had to go somewhere, I figured it might as well be there. I didn't choose the earliest possible flight, though. I picked September 11, 2005, hoping to create a positive association with that date.

Searching for a job and an apartment in mid-life in an unfamiliar city wasn't easy. Despite the friends I've made here in the Pacific Northwest, and finding a wonderful, loving husband, I lost something when Katrina hit. I lost my past. I lost most of my circle of friends. I lost a world I knew and loved.

But not evacuating wouldn't have changed that. The hurricane was on a collision course. Even though it weakened before making landfall, the destruction was unavoidable by that point. My choice wasn't whether to keep the life I had or to evacuate. The choice was to evacuate or become another of the hurricane's many victims.

Choosing not to address the climate crisis won't stop the devastation heading our way. Building new pipelines and storage facilities and drilling new wells won't weaken the storm bearing down on us. If anything, such decisions will only ensure it remains a category 5 at landfall.

The grocery store that served my New Orleans neighborhood only opened again in 2019, fourteen years after it was destroyed. Yes, there will be survivors of climate crisis even if we do nothing, but they won't have a functioning infrastructure for a very long time. Much longer than fourteen years.

Addressing climate crisis head-on won't be easy. We'll be snarled in traffic jams so stressful we'll want to turn back. And we'll only be able bring part of our lives with us. We are going to lose much that is important to us, much that we love.

Two of my friends refused to evacuate for Katrina because they couldn't bring their five pets with them. Luana and Margie were eventually rescued from their second-floor balcony by helicopter. They had to leave four of their pets behind.

Not "evacuating" won't keep the devastation of climate change away. The only survivable option is to grab what we can, try to save as much of our civilization and ecosystem as we are able, and flee for our lives in stop-and-go traffic.

Lots of people burned to death in their cars trying to escape the climate-driven wildfires in Paradise last year. But not evacuating wouldn't have saved their lives. At least some of those who fled made it out.

A climate emergency is here. Ignoring it won't make it go away. We must take drastic action to save what we can. Our lives will not be the same any longer. We either accept that. Or we die.

A Barbed Wire Tightrope

We used to encourage refugees to come to America. I remember in elementary school my teacher showing our class a film of East Germans seeking freedom from Communist tyranny. I watched as a young couple ran for their lives from East Berlin to the West before the wall was completed. They raced at full speed right into a barbed wire fence, too desperate to slow themselves down even knowing the jagged wires were ahead.

I watched as the couple tried to pull their clothes and skin free of the barbs so they could claw their way through the barrier before the soldiers firing could stop them permanently. I was deeply affected by the real-life drama unfolding on the screen, witnessing proof of how wonderful America was. I was blessed to live in the Land of the Free.

Years later, I saw *Man on a Tightrope* on Turner Classic Movies. The film is a fictionalized version of a true story involving an Eastern European circus troupe that defects together to the West. The climax, with the circus performers running across a bridge with bullets flying after them, still makes me tremble, still causes my vision to blur.

Back then, Americans *wanted* to offer people a better life. We liked knowing we were the country people came to because we and they and everyone knew we were the best. Einstein came to the U.S. Maria von Trapp came to the U.S. Irving Berlin and Madeline Albright came as well.

We even wanted nobodies like those represented by Barbra Streisand in *Yentl*. Neil Diamond, singing about taxi drivers and cooks and others of low social status, triumphantly declared, "They're coming to America!" This was the place to be, and we celebrated it.

But somewhere along the way, we decided that people being raped and imprisoned and killed in their home countries deserved what they got for being stupid enough to be born there, for being rude enough not to speak English as their first language.

Yes, there's long been resistance, too. Quotas. And the infamous turning away of *The Voyage of the Damned*. But by and large, we agreed so much with Emma Lazarus—Give me your tired, your poor, your huddled masses yearning to breathe free—that we put this Jewish woman's words on the Statue of Liberty.

Refugees aren't immigrants—they're defecting from countries ruled by dictators, poverty, gangs, civil war, and drought. Christians and capitalists run toward us as fast as they can, young couples, mothers and fathers carrying their children, young teens, even old men and women. They race forward desperately, so afraid of what's behind them that they crash full speed into the barrier that is us.

We've become the barbed wire ripping people apart and denying them access to freedom.

If we could demand that Gorbachev tear down the Berlin wall, we can demand that our own leaders cut through barbed wire.

Or perhaps we can settle for a Czech or Hungarian or Romanian film: *Make America the Iron Curtain Again.* We can see the daily rushes every evening even now on the nightly news.

And I can see Joan Crawford shaking a flag, screaming, "No more defections!" as refugee children cower in terror.

Ah, nostalgia. Where is Frank Capra when you need him?

Chicken Little: One if by Land, Two if by Sea

(published in *LA Progressive* on 5 May 2019)

When an acorn fell on Chicken Little's head, she began running around warning her fellow chickens. "The sky is falling! The sky is falling!"

For years, climate activists have been doing the same thing, running about frantically, trying to save their friends from the danger fast approaching. But politicians, and the voters who put them in office, think no more of us than they do of Chicken Little.

Now when I read another account of present (not future) climate disaster, I'm actually a little bit happy. If warnings are not enough, perhaps consequences will be.

A native of New Orleans, I grew up knowing that flooding was "normal." One evening, when I heard a particularly heavy downpour, I told my partner, "That's a flooding rain." I looked outside to see if the streets were clear. They were. My car was safe.

When the 10:00 news came on, the first story was, "Major flooding throughout the city." I ran back to the door and looked outside again. It was already too late. Water was halfway up the car door. Within moments, it was coming in the house. Fourteen inches of rain fell in just two hours.

Back then, when I told other people from different parts of the country about that evening (it got worse), they didn't believe me.

Today, 25 years later, people believe me without protest. Events of extreme precipitation happen often in many other places these days.

Along with more frequent flooding, we have more frequent droughts and wildfires. While it was heartbreaking to see Paradise, California obliterated, part of me felt relieved. Maybe now people would understand what we're up against if we don't take drastic action.

But no, we still don't get it. We can't pass a Green New Deal in Congress. In Washington state, where the governor's bid for the presidency is based on action to address climate change, we can't even ban fracking or new pipelines.

When the American Midwest experienced catastrophic flooding in the spring of 2019, I was...happy.

It's an awful thing to say, isn't it? I remember some of my relatives being happy when I contracted HIV. Maybe now I would repent and stop being gay. Their happiness on my behalf did not feel as loving as they seemed to believe it was.

So, yes, maybe I'm an ass. I can live with that.

The past two summers in Seattle, smoke from wildfires hundreds of miles away made our air so thick with particulate matter we could often see no farther than two blocks. The news reported almost every day that our air quality was Very Unhealthy. Other days, it was Hazardous.

Almost 20% of coral reefs around the world have died in the past few decades. 15% more will likely die within the next 15 years. Another 20% will follow in the 20 years after that. Within 35 more years, we will have lost 75% of coral reefs around the world.

Indonesia has committed to moving its capital from Jakarta to a city deeper inland. In the next 30 or so years, 95% of Jakarta will be under water.

30 years sounds like a number too large and unreliable to worry about. But it's not the distant future. 14 years have already passed since Hurricane Katrina forced me to relocate thousands of miles from my hometown, and I still feel like a newcomer in Seattle.

An addict often won't seek treatment until he or she hits rock bottom. Apparently, we need to sink even deeper into the gutter of climate disaster. I keep hoping the next algae bloom or wildfire or flood or hurricane will finally open our hearts to an intervention.

What's most mystifying to me is why conservatives complain that combating climate change will cost too much.

Yes, tackling carbon emissions is expensive, but that just means *someone is going to make money*. Conservatives, don't you want it to be you?

Someone is going to make money developing and selling solar energy technology and products. *Someone* is going to make money developing and selling wind power technology and products. The same for wave energy and thermal energy and carbon capture.

Doesn't the Party of business want to get in on this? Promote commerce? Make millions from advances through Research and Development? In retrofitting homes and businesses?

These changes will *have* to be made sooner or later. Why not be the ones to corner the market now? The sooner we develop the products and technology, the sooner we'll make money.

Of course, we'll not only *make* money, but we'll also help limit future *losses*. Burned and flooded homes, the relocation of residents and businesses, and the widespread loss of crops all cost billions. Those losses will only increase if we don't act quickly and drastically.

Fiscal conservatives should be on board solely out of self-interest.

But they're addicted to the drugs they're on now, fossil fuels and the money derived from them. So I keep hoping the next disaster will hurt enough people to make a difference.

Being Chicken Little, or even Paul Revere warning of danger by land or by sea, doesn't seem to be enough.

Sometimes, when a couple realize they need to divorce, they put it off because of the hassle in finding lawyers, dividing the assets, the cost of finding a new place to live. It's all too emotionally and financially overwhelming.

But delaying the inevitable because it's hard only prolongs the misery. We can't start building the new life we need till we finally face reality and do the hard work that must be done.

I see on the news tonight that lawmakers are still refusing to address climate change. But there's hope. Tomorrow when I turn on the TV, maybe I'll see a report about another catastrophic flood. Hurricane season starts soon, too. And wildfire season is just around the corner.

I'll keep my fingers crossed and hope the people I love won't die before they get into recovery.

When Protesting against Genocide Is a Racist Act

(published in the *Salt Lake Tribune* on 12 May 2019)

Some of my Mormon friends and relatives post frequently about the atrocity of racial genocide. But, like many white conservatives of the religious right, the only racial injustice they seem able to see anywhere in the world is that heaped upon whites by people of color.

My friends and relatives sound the alarm regularly about blacks killing whites, recently posting a photo of several black Africans in South Africa marching with white baby dolls nailed to posts, quite a horrifying image.

Still, I admit to feeling ambivalent about their repeated calls for justice. It's like a police officer ticketing a black driver for speeding. Yes, the driver was breaking the law, but when *only* black drivers get ticketed in a given county or principality, while white drivers speed on by, the enforcement of a law we all agree is good becomes a racist act, not the embodiment of justice.

My Mormon friends and relatives, like so many other conservatives, don't protest when white police officers kill unarmed blacks. I don't hear a word from them about the multiple documented cases of voter suppression, when ballots collected from black voters are discarded, or polling places in majority black areas are eliminated. My conservative Mormon friends and family don't protest against President Trump's Muslim ban, or about Israeli atrocities against Palestinians. I don't hear a word in support of desperate immigrants and refugees trying to enter the Promised Land.

But if a white person anywhere in the world is hurt or killed by non-whites, *that's* worth talking about.

And it *is*.

But when they don't talk about oppression and violence against whites when it is perpetrated by other whites, I can't quite believe their sense of outrage isn't tinged with racism. I don't hear my conservative Mormon friends and relatives protesting Wal-Mart's low wages forcing thousands of its white employees to apply for food stamps and other government assistance.

I don't hear any complaints about a for-profit healthcare system that refuses care to millions of white people, leading to tens of thousands of premature white deaths every year. I hear nothing when a white domestic terrorist kills dozens of whites at a country music concert, a single act which killed more whites than all the white farmers killed in South Africa last year.

But liberals and progressives are awful because they don't care about white genocide in South Africa!

Yes, we care about the murder of white people. It's just not the *only* thing we care about. We care that even after the end of apartheid, South Africa remains a nation with perhaps the most extreme income inequality in the world.

Closer to home, we care about conservatives removing elected officials in Flint, Michigan and poisoning its water supply. We care that, years later, the problem still hasn't been resolved. I haven't heard any of my religious conservative relatives say a word in support of reparations for the descendants of African slaves. I haven't heard them say anything *against* reparations, either. The issue is completely unimportant to them.

That's a problem.

On Columbus Day, one of my Mormon relatives posted about how brutal Native Americans were, that they gave as good as they got, so he was going to celebrate Columbus, not indigenous people. Mormons, who revere the Book of Mormon as scripture written by Native Americans, should instinctively care a little more about indigenous people, but right-wing racism has beaten back their theology and compassion like an angry mob.

If the only injustices my right-wing friends and family care about are those which afford them the opportunity to demonize blacks or other people of color, it's difficult not to see their protests against genocide as a racist act. Especially when they offer no suggestions for how to resolve the racial problems in South Africa or anywhere else. The point of the posts I see is simply that blacks are bad and white people are the real victims in today's world of political correctness.

We don't need to compete for whose injuries are worse. We should be able to unite and together fight injustice everywhere we see it. We on the left are willing to side with conservatives when they are oppressed, with whites when they are oppressed, with anyone anywhere who is oppressed. But to be successful, we're going to need religious conservatives to care about justice for more than just themselves.

Let's work together to make the world a safer place for everyone.

Payday Loans Suck Life from the Poor

(published in *LA Progressive* on 20 May 2019)

I lost my job at the New Orleans public library when Hurricane Katrina devastated the city, and I relocated to Seattle. The first job I could find was with a check cashing and payday loan company. But what at first felt like a blessing soon turned into a nightmare.

When I was a kid, I loved Barnabas Collins. I watched the daytime soap *Dark Shadows* every day as soon as I got home from school. Quentin the werewolf was great, Kate Jackson as Daphne in her first television role was captivating, and what kid couldn't identify with young David, who talked to the ghost of his dead cousin Sarah? But Barnabas was the best character in the series. I made my mother buy me a ring like his, asked her to find me a cane like his. I wanted to be Barnabas.

When I saw the soap opera again decades later, I was shocked to discover that Barnabas was the villain of the show. I already knew he was a vampire, of course, but instead of a poor, misunderstood hero, he was a cruel and manipulative killer. He bit Willie and Carolyn and turned them into slaves forced to serve him against their own best interests. Barnabas was not the good guy.

I've heard people say that payday loans offer financial assistance to those no one else will help, so whatever their drawbacks, payday loan companies are offering the poor a real service. But let me tell you what I saw.

Poor, desperate people came to us around the clock. When I worked the graveyard shift, I was amazed at the folks who would come in at 3:00 in the morning for a loan. What in the world was going on in their lives that a payday loan at that hour was their only option?

Of course, the fact that it *was* their only option is the point. People don't willingly choose to have a foot amputated. An economic system that forces the poor through the doors of a payday loan store are essentially "serving" a segment of society that have developed gangrene, people who have been deliberately injected with *Clostridium perfringens* so others can profit from "treating" them.

Our customers frequently demonstrated behavioral problems. There was the man who came in to urinate in the trash can in our lobby. There were the two young women who talked about the most humane way to get people addicted to drugs so that the two women would have a steady income. Then there was the guy who came in with his jeans down around his knees, and no underwear to make up for the displaced attire.

"Uh, sir," I said, "you're going to need to pull up your pants."

"I can't," he stated matter-of-factly. "I shit in them."

At that moment, I could smell he was telling the truth. I started working quickly to cash his check. As I did, I saw a young, clean-cut couple enter the store, newbies rather than regulars. I saw the horror on their faces as they stared at the backside of the man at my window. The couple retreated quickly.

But they returned thirty seconds later. Shit or no shit, they needed money.

Another afternoon, a young black woman came to my window. She was gentle and polite, which was certainly not the norm among our clientele. When she handed over her paystubs along with her payment, I saw immediately that her stubs were too old for us to use to make another loan. 90% of our customers who repaid a loan took out another one at the same time. They were almost never able to pay off their debt and go back to a "normal" life.

I knew that if the young woman was aware I was not going to be able to extend another loan that she would keep her money and pay us back later. But my boss told me to take the money. It was due that day, and the customer's problems weren't our concern. So I took the money. And as I gave her the receipt, I informed her we couldn't reloan with the documents she'd given us.

The young woman did not protest. She did not become angry. She just nodded sadly and went to sit in one of our chairs in the lobby, where she lowered her head and cried softly. She'd told me when she arrived that her rent was due that day.

What the hell was wrong with me? How could I let my own financial struggles persuade me to aid and abet the monsters running this company?

If "just following orders" wasn't good enough for the Nazis on trial at Nuremburg, it wasn't good enough for me. I searched harder for another job and finally found one, but there will always be a stain on my soul from the time I spent assisting vampires as they preyed on the poor.

I do remember several other of my check cashing customers even all these years later. The alcoholic who came in scraped up because he kept falling on the sidewalk while intoxicated. The homeless man who wanted to become my lover. I remember the guy who told me that as bad as we were, we were better than banks. At least our fees were up front.

To adequately address the abuses of payday loan and check cashing stores, we must also address the multiple issues in mainstream banking.

We must stop thinking of Barnabas Collins as the hero. We need to put the bloodsucking payday loan industry into its coffin, and then nail the lid shut.

A wooden stake would do, too.

Let's end our enslavement to those who operate in the shadows and move into the sunshine instead.

Eyes in the Back of My Head

(published in *Main Street Plaza* on 19 May 2019)

In the life of every atheist raised in a religious household, there comes a moment when we encounter our first question that can't be answered. For me, it was when, as a young Mormon teen reading science fiction novels, I encountered aliens with amazing abilities. I'd think, "Wouldn't it be great if humans had *that* feature?" Nature programs added non-fiction traits other species already had, species inferior to God—according to God—yet obviously superior in some of their physical attributes. If God was the ultimate being, how could that be?

Why, for instance, didn't humans display more attractive coloring? Blue, red, green, purple? We were mostly drab beiges and browns. We colored our hair and tattooed ourselves and wore flashy clothes because we instinctively understood the need to improve upon nature.

When I was trying to nail or tape or cut something, I'd think, "Boy, wouldn't it be great to have an extra arm or two?" I thought about how convenient it would be to tell ourselves, "Put your finger there so I can tie this."

Something wasn't right.

When bullies crept up behind me at school, how could I not wonder why humans, made in the image of a perfect God, didn't have eyes in the back of our head?

Why did we have unprotected shins?

If shivering generated heat when we were cold, why did people who still had adequate stores of fat freeze to death before burning up their reserves?

Why couldn't we breathe in both air and water?

Why couldn't we fly?

Why couldn't we regenerate lost appendages?

Why didn't we have a mouth on the end of some new appendage that we could manipulate more freely than we could move our head?

I had lots of questions, but the biggest was why a being that clearly didn't have the best of all possible bodies was still able to label itself the Supreme Being in the universe. And if we as Mormons had the opportunity to become gods ourselves, with the same bodies we had on Earth, only "perfected," wasn't it a bit unfair that we beat out other species that scored so much higher on any objective evaluation of overall traits?

Something wasn't right.

Of course, I would eventually decide that the issue of physical attributes was the least of the problems most theologians created.

Why, for instance, did other animals and insects need to suffer when their moral character wasn't being tested to determine if they qualified for godhood? They just suffered.

Why was suffering the only method for helping humans progress to the next level? The most intelligent being in the entire universe couldn't come up with anything better than that? If God himself is bound by "natural" laws, who made up those laws? Atoms and molecules did that all by themselves?

The questions didn't stop there. After reaching a certain threshold, though, there wasn't much point even asking anything else.

Despite the dangers of unregulated genetic manipulation, I now accept that our fate is in our own hands, and we have to be proactive in ensuring our advancement. Perhaps soon we can create features to turn us into the superior beings we want to be. More intelligent, more compassionate, more altruistic. Maybe we'll be able to individually choose specific genes for ourselves. On the issue of sex alone, I can think of quite a few improvements I could make to my body.

Don't tell me you don't have a fantasy wish list, too.

The possibilities are as endless as the number of people out there.

But no, we're stuck with two eyes, two arms, two legs, and—sadly—just the one penis.

If God is the most intelligent, most powerful being in the universe, why can't *he* figure out safe genetic engineering?

I don't need Noah's flood to make me doubt. I don't need anachronisms in the Book of Mormon. I don't need any of the vast multitude of theological issues debated regularly to open my eyes to the implausibility of God's existence. The eyes in the front of my head are enough for that.

What Have You Got against a Stable Climate?

Many of the conservatives in my life aren't worried about the climate crisis because the news they watch and the people they respect tell them all is well. My sister, my niece and nephews, my aunt and cousins, my former Mormon bishop, and my other friends from church all hear the same propaganda. "The Earth has been much hotter during its lifetime. A little warming is no big deal."

What, I respond when I hear such things, have you got against a stable climate?

It's true enough that at times the Earth's climate has been warmer than it is today. We can concede that for the first 700 million years of its existence, our planet's surface was mostly molten lava. No big deal, right?

4.5 billion years is a long time, and the planet's surface has experienced widely varying temperatures during its history. Manhattan under a mile of ice is no big deal, either, I suppose.

No climate activists are denying that there have been shifts in global temperatures in the Earth's past. Most dinosaurs, except the branch that became birds, died when temperatures plummeted after a meteorite impact. That was the planet's fifth mass extinction. Of course, temperature change isn't the only factor driving the current mass extinction event, but virtually all of the other factors are man-made as well.

After Mt. Tambora erupted in 1815, the following year was labeled "the year without summer." Crops failed across Europe. Famines and riots claimed 200,000 lives.

That was a one-year period of climate disruption.

I've heard conservatives complain that people pushing action on climate change are only doing it because it's "good business and gives scientists jobs."

What have they got against good business and jobs?

Granted, many of us don't like the economic and physical destruction caused by some corporations, and we don't like jobs that hurt people or endanger other species. But what damage is being done by the business and jobs of climate activists? A coal miner loses the opportunity to develop black lung disease?

Coal mining is quickly going extinct regardless of climate change. People no longer earn a living from opening elevator doors, either. Jobs are lost to cultural changes, automation, and outsourcing all the time. We certainly do need stronger programs to train people for career change, but complaining that solar energy employees and scientists are stealing our jobs is not an effective strategy for accomplishing that.

I have to wonder why those who refuse to act on climate change are so against the Earth having a stable climate, or at least as stable a climate as we can manage. What does that gain them?

I keep remembering Lex Luthor's plan in the first *Superman* movie. He wanted to set off nuclear bombs that would cause everything west of the San Andreas fault to sink into the ocean. Luthor bought up thousands of acres of land just to the east so that he'd have prime real estate after his man-made adjustment to the coastline.

I can't help but wonder who might be buying up properties inland from Miami, Ft. Lauderdale, St. Petersburg, Daytona Beach, Tallahassee, and all the other coastal cities in Florida that will disappear over the next few decades.

We can debate approaches for addressing the climate crisis, but dismissing the need for a stable climate altogether is like saying we don't need a stable stock market, that we don't need stoplights or laws against stealing and killing. Chaos and destruction are *not* good for business or jobs. They're not good for orangutans or polar bears or palm trees. They're not good for coastal cities around the world and the hundreds of millions of people who live in them.

And they're not good, I'm afraid, even for the conservatives we love who naïvely say climate change is no big deal.

Mandatory Courses on Race, Gender, and Social Justice

(published in *LA Progressive* on 23 November 2018 and reprinted in *Dead Mankind Walking*)

Every degree from every accredited college, university, or trade school must include at least one mandatory course on race, gender, and social justice. There is no field in which students and workers do not need to understand the history of discrimination and the ways oppression still occurs in virtually every work environment in America.

I grew up in New Orleans, with extended family in rural Mississippi. As a child, I was given Confederate caps and flags to play with. When we visited Vicksburg, my mother told me, "Oh, don't look at THAT monument. It's for Yankees. Ooh! Look at THIS monument! It's for US!"

I also grew up Mormon, in my late teens before the LDS Church "allowed" Blacks to hold the priesthood. Women still can't.

As a gay man whose personal politics grew increasingly progressive throughout my adulthood, I am still woefully ignorant of the history of oppression and of ways to diminish institutional racism and sexism and all the other types of discrimination which occur throughout society.

I earned one Biology and three English degrees. While literature helped me understand other cultures and social classes a bit more, there was never any instruction specifically on race and gender. I had to pick up little snippets here and there. I also taught at a Black university for ten years. An eye-opening experience, I still only caught brief glimpses of my unintentional but still harmful bias and discriminatory behavior. Random learning isn't sufficient.

I found myself shocked by the racism and sexism I witnessed among some of my gay friends in New Orleans, disturbed that so many people seemed unable to transform their own suffering into understanding the suffering of others.

After relocating to liberal Seattle in the wake of Hurricane Katrina, a disaster which itself taught me more about racism, I married another ex-Mormon who believed in social justice. My husband became involved in Socialist politics, and I volunteered with Radical Women. But because my work schedule didn't allow me time to take actual coursework, I still only learned bits and pieces.

I recently watched "Hidden Figures," horrified to witness a scientist who wasn't allowed to use the bathroom in her building. Instead, she had to run half a mile, in heels, sometimes in the rain, every time she needed to pee. How did I not already know about this demeaning, humiliating, everyday oppression?

My current employer feels it important to address racial and social justice. Every employee is required to participate in an all-day training. I also chose to take three additional half-day trainings—Implicit Bias I, Implicit Bias II, and Internalized Racial Superiority. I was astonished to learn that the Irish were not considered white during part of American history, that Finnish people weren't considered white. It reinforced my understanding of race as a social construct, but I realized immediately I needed an entire semester of such instruction, at the very least. If I had reached the age of 57 without knowing these basic facts, how much more history did I, a reasonably well-educated adult, know nothing about?

A Black co-worker asked me why I was taking this training. "Because I don't want to be an asshole," I replied. "Or at least be less of one."

Yes, we could all study on our own, but the realities of life prevent that from actually happening, even for people who want to learn. And it's just as important, perhaps more so, that people who aren't interested in learning about these issues do so anyway. Something so essential to the success and security of our nation can't be left to chance, any more than we would allow citizens to choose whether or not they felt personally compelled to pay their income tax, or to get a driver's license before sitting behind the wheel of a car.

If our country is ever going to be truly post-racial, ever truly cease its misogyny and finally treat all people equally regardless of color, gender, orientation, religion, or anything else, then everyone must learn about these issues, much earlier and more fully than I have. Some of this history should be introduced in middle school and high school, and taught in even more depth in every accredited institution of higher learning. People in every field of study or work must understand oppression and ways to reduce our complicity in continuing it.

Mandatory courses on race, gender, and social justice should be prerequisites for graduation into society because everyone, even those already enjoying privilege, will benefit both financially and emotionally once all people are treated with equal respect, humanity, and justice.

Don't Feed the Humans: Criminalizing Compassion

(published in the *Orlando Sentinel* on 18 June 2019)

In recent months, government agents have begun implementing a new tactic to deny illegal immigrants and desperate refugees the opportunity to find a safe haven in the U.S. In addition to arresting and detaining immigrants, even those entering legally and making legal requests for asylum, government agencies have begun arresting anyone daring to provide food or water to those crossing one of the most dangerous deserts in our hemisphere. We're not talking about forcing volunteer aid workers to pay a nuisance fine. These humanitarians are being charged with felonies and face up to twenty years in prison.

Agents claim that providing water to a pregnant woman is an act of human smuggling. Of course, no one is fooled by this attempt at spinning the narrative. While actual human smuggling may rightly be condemned, offering compassion shouldn't be criminalized. When charges of smuggling appear too ridiculous to sustain, agents switch to another charge. They arrest humanitarians providing water with littering and abandonment of property.

A zero-tolerance policy against littering in the Sonoran desert might be more believable if deliberate government shutdowns didn't allow mountains of garbage to accumulate in our parks, if oil and toxic chemicals weren't contaminating many of our rivers, lakes, and coastal waters, if city streets weren't overflowing with trash all across the country. In the impoverished White Center neighborhood where I work, just inches outside Seattle city limits, public trash cans have been set up in multiple locations, but there is no regular pick up. For the past three years I've worked in the area, I've seen garbage overflowing from every can. Birds pick through it. Homeless people pick through it. Undocumented immigrants, I suspect, pick through it as well.

It's almost as if the purpose of the trash cans isn't to keep the area clean but to offer proof that the destitute cause their own problems. "These people are animals. Look at the filth they live in." Poor and homeless people obviously don't have the capacity to cart off garbage from public receptacles to the appropriate government facilities. But this denial of sanitary conditions to the poor isn't accidental. It's not an oversight. It's an effective way to dehumanize. Poor people just aren't worth the nominal funds it would take to empty their trash cans, and they hear that message loud and clear.

But by golly, if someone hands a dehydrated child a plastic jug of water that might be left behind in the desert, we must do whatever is necessary to stamp out such reckless behavior!

That child may not understand English, but she hears the message America is sending her just as clearly—our zero-tolerance policies give her a zero-value life.

Even if there were some way to justify the criminalization of humanitarian aid to non-citizens, there seems to be even less justification for arresting people in dozens of cities across the U.S. who offer food to our steadily increasing homeless population. Government officials claim these laws are designed to prevent the spread of disease, but one wonders why, if the health of homeless men, women, and children is their primary concern, these same officials don't ensure that health by distributing food through "appropriate" means, furnishing adequate shelter, or, at the very least, offering guaranteed healthcare. Providing medical services, after all, seems like a better way to safeguard health than denying them food.

No one is deceived by the pretense that criminalizing aid to the poor, destitute, and dying is to "protect" the vulnerable. The goal is clearly to penalize empathy, drive compassion into the closet, make good, decent people afraid to act humanely toward their fellow man. If people are forced to worry enough about themselves, are made to fear banding together to help one another, they are easier to control.

"Intellectuals" are among the first to be imprisoned when totalitarian governments rise to power. Humanitarians seem to be near the top of the list as well, at least for our totalitarian-wannabe leaders. When "Don't Feed the Humans" becomes the moral equivalent of "Don't Feed the Pigeons," we know we are in serious trouble.

To protect our nation's standing in the world, to protect the character of our citizens, and to protect human life itself, we must stop criminalizing compassion.

Addiction to Money and Power Is a Public Health Crisis

HIV, Ebola, influenza, heart disease, and cancer combined pale in comparison to the world's most serious health crisis. We must fund research to create better ways to treat—and hopefully one day cure—addiction. While alcohol, nicotine, meth, and opioid addictions are the first that come to mind, even they fall far short of the most devastating addictions of all, the addictions to money and power.

We must stop behaving as if the insatiable hunger for money and power are character flaws. The nicest, kindest, most loving people in the world can become monsters when caught up in drug addiction, and the same is true for the addiction to money and power.

These two addictions are the primary cause of virtually all suffering on the planet. No addiction to money? Then we all get a non-profit healthcare system. No addiction to power? Then we get leaders trying to solve problems rather than score points.

A friend of mine in recovery for over twenty years told me the moment he realized he had a problem. Walking down the street, he saw a half-filled beer bottle on someone's lawn being used to attract and drown slugs. My friend paused a few moments to consider if he wanted that beer enough that he'd be willing to drink it even if there were dead slugs in it.

J. Paul Getty was asked why he didn't feel secure even though he had more money than anyone in human history had ever possessed. "What would it take for you to feel secure?"

His answer? "More."

That's not a character flaw. It's an addiction.

This is not to say that people addicted to money and power don't have plenty of actual character flaws as well, but it's the addiction that is the real issue. In his first epistle to Timothy, when Paul said, "The LOVE of money is the root of all evil," he showed an understanding of this basic physiological vulnerability.

Given the millions of people who die every year as a direct result of actions of the rich and powerful, the addiction to money and power is perhaps the most important health crisis facing humanity.

If we want to mitigate climate change, we must find a way to treat addiction to money and power.

If we want everyone to receive a good education and adequate healthcare, we must find a way to treat addiction to money and power.

If we want to eliminate sexism and racism, if we want to stop war, we must find a way to treat addiction to money and power.

We can try to create laws and enforce them, but those only address symptoms, not the disease itself. We can try to elect the best politicians. But even good people, once they become addicts, will often sell their souls to feed their addiction.

My doctor prescribed Desonide lotion to treat my dermatitis. I've used the lotion for twenty years. It works great. But maintaining clear skin requires constant vigilance. If I skip three or four days, the red, scaly patches develop on my face overnight, and it can take several days of regular treatment to get my skin back under control. Then I must maintain constant vigilance again.

Because we're treating the symptoms, not the disease causing them.

My year-round allergies give me a runny and stuffy nose. I've taken two or three antihistamines every day for the past thirty years. They work well. But if I forget to take a pill the instant I wake up in the morning, a cascade of reactions in my body advances too quickly for me to resolve with a pill or two, and it may take several more hours to get my body back under control. Achieving normal breathing is a daily battle requiring non-stop monitoring.

Because we're treating the symptoms, not the disease.

Addiction to money and power isn't a metaphor. It's a physiological problem, and we must make finding a cure one of our top priorities. Otherwise, we'll never be able to meet any of our other needs.

The researchers who accomplish this great service to mankind will likely be awarded the Nobel Prize in Medicine simultaneously with the Nobel Peace Prize.

Addiction to money and power is a disease. The Manhattan Project, the Race to the Moon, and a Green New Deal give us a taste of the commitment necessary to tackle this problem successfully. The race to recovery will have a direct impact on the extent of the 6th mass extinction event currently underway, the only extinction event in the history of the planet caused by a single species rather than a global disaster.

Let's find a cure before it's too late.

Life, Liberty, and the Pursuit of Unhappiness

"Making a law banning assault weapons isn't going to change anything. Criminals will always find a way to break the law."

While even the majority of gun owners want universal background checks and greater regulation of assault-type weapons, Republican leaders who represent them insist there's no point making any laws to reduce mass murder because shooters will keep doing it, anyway.

I wonder, then, why these same conservatives want to make more laws regulating voting. If voters are going to commit fraud anyway, why insist on photo IDs?

Why insist on criminalizing abortion? People are going to keep having abortions anyway.

Why insist on criminalizing crossing the border? People are going to cross the border anyway.

And as far as that goes, why act internationally to stop North Korea or Iran from getting nuclear weapons? Other countries are going to develop nuclear weapons anyway. And we all know it isn't nukes that kill people, it's people who kill people.

Those committed to "defending" the Second Amendment instead want to rewrite the Declaration of Independence to demand "the right to life, liberty, and the pursuit of taking life and liberty from others."

Retrofitting Notre Dame

When a friend of mine posted a picture on Facebook of the new roof proposed for Notre Dame in Paris, I saw comments like, "It's ghastly!" and "Is this satire?" There was a "what is the world coming to?" feel to the responses, but only in the sense of good taste. No one seemed to recognize that a roof full of solar panels and a garden to raise food for the poor was exactly the kind of repairs we should be making when important structures are damaged. In fact, we should also mandate that all existing homes and businesses be retrofitted with features to combat global warming, and that all new construction require it from the start.

When my husband and I bought a 1906 Craftsman cottage in south Seattle, we knew it would require upgrades, renovation, and repairs. That's what people *expect* when dealing with old homes. The first order of business was to replace the front door. For a hundred years, that door consisted of 15 panes of glass. It offered no privacy, no protection against the heat or cold, and, we soon discovered, no protection against burglary. We now have a front door made of thick pine planks. It doesn't completely fit the style of the home, but we had to make this practical adjustment. That's what living in today's world demands.

The next project on our Craftsman cottage, far larger, was to install insulation in the walls and ceiling. No one would even consider building a new home today without this basic feature. We removed the coal-burning furnace. We retrofitted our home to make it more earthquake-resistant by anchoring the walls to the foundation. We replaced eight single-pane windows with energy-efficient ones.

The bathroom in our lovely home isn't the best, but it's better than the one original to the property—an outhouse in the back yard. Just as no one today would consider purchasing an existing house or constructing a new one without a functioning bathroom, we must adjust our expectations of what is essential. Would we build a new home in the suburbs of Atlanta without installing air conditioning? Central air and heating may not be cheap, but we accept that it's a necessary expense.

Upgrading all homes and businesses to address the climate crisis is just as necessary.

But that proposal for a new roof on Notre Dame with its spire of solar panels? Is that really where we need to go?

I don't think I will ever like the Pompidou Centre in Paris, a monstrosity of modern design surrounded by all the beautiful and traditional architecture of the 4th arrondissement. I will never like the glass pyramid in front of the Louvre blocking my view of the museum. But changes in style can't be avoided as our cultures evolve over time, regardless of climate concerns. And when those changes do involve the realities of global warming, we are just going to have to live with them.

During the 1980's, the world faced a danger it had never encountered before. Bathhouses started distributing condoms to slow the spread of HIV, but many men didn't want to use them. The porn industry rose to the challenge and required adult films to show men wearing condoms to make them sexier. Porn stories in magazines were required to describe characters engaging in safer sex. The entire industry worked to change the cultural norms that were killing people.

Most guys still don't *like* condoms. They use them because survival requires it.

I don't like injecting myself with insulin twice a day. I do it because I want to make it to my next birthday.

Few people enjoy colonoscopies, but we don't submit to them for fun. We do it to avoid early, preventable death.

Not every human on the planet is going to die as global temperatures continue to rise. We won't go extinct. But is losing "only" a few hundred million people, or a few billion, with the survivors suffering the cataclysms of inundated cities, crop losses and famine, and the resulting wars over resources, really the *best* way to save money? And is saving money really the *best* goal we can have?

Wouldn't it be better to replace outhouses with indoor plumbing, thin walls with insulation, and inefficient windows with efficient ones?

Notre Dame won't look the same with a solar panel roof. But after the fire, looking the same was no longer an option in any event. Just as status quo construction codes are no longer an option. Retrofitting existing structures and demanding more of new construction are not luxuries. They're essential.

The sooner we adapt to the reality of our new circumstances, the better off we, the buildings we love, and the planet we all live on, will be.

Does the Second Anointing Explain Mormon Support for Trump?

(published in *Main Street Plaza* on 23 August 2019)

I am baffled that so many Mormons support Donald Trump. At one point, the percentage of Mormon Trump supporters was the highest of any religion (61% according to a 2017 Gallup poll). While some Mormon opposition has existed from the start, the vast majority of Mormons heartily endorsed a man who admitted groping women, who mocked a disabled reporter, who called on followers to assault his opponents, and who, by anyone's definition, was a great big creep.

I speak Italian, as a result of my time as a Mormon missionary in Rome, and I've studied French, Spanish, Russian, Hebrew, and American Sign Language. I also took a translation course in grad school. When I hear so many Mormons say, "No one's perfect. But Trump has good policies," I'm able to translate that pretty easily.

What they're really saying is, "You can commit any sin as long as you are serving God while doing so."

Almost all Mormons are fine with Nephi killing and robbing a drunk, sleeping Laban. Too many Mormons are fine with covering up sexual abuse "to protect the name of the Church." And an uncomfortably large number are fine with a history of racist prophets because those prophets "were only human."

While people in general have the capacity to excuse the abuse of others as long as they themselves aren't abused, Mormon theology has a specific teaching that makes accepting bad behavior part of God's plan. Once a person receives "the Second Anointing," that person has their Calling and Election made sure and is guaranteed a spot in the Celestial Kingdom, no matter what sins he or she may commit after that. They are like international diplomats who can't be prosecuted for crimes they commit in other countries. They have permanent amnesty. Mormons who've had the Second Anointing can literally get away with murder. Or with shooting someone on Fifth Avenue. They possess a "Get Out of Judgment Day Free" card.

Perhaps this also explains why two Mormons were among the top contributors to the U.S. military torture program.

Many Mormons in the U.S. honestly don't care about any of Trump's "personal" failings because, even if he isn't a member of the Church, the principle is the same. He's lowering taxes, he's banning transgender folks from the military, and he's Making America Great Again. That's more than just a campaign slogan for Mormons, whose theology insists that America is the Promised Land, reserved for the righteous and the righteous alone. If Trump can get rid of some of the undesirables, he's doing God's bidding. If he must be cruel and oppressive and criminal to do it, well, they can live with that.

The Second Anointing basically teaches Mormons that those at the top are not subject to the same rules and laws that the rest of us must obey. So when Trump says he's exempt from prosecution for absolutely *anything*, Mormons have been trained to accept that declaration as reasonable.

"Lying for the Lord" is a common Mormon practice, so why shouldn't "Imprisoning Legal Asylum Seekers for the Lord" be an acceptable practice as well? And "Oppressing Workers for the Lord" and "Bankrupting Farmers for the Lord" and "Befriending Murderous Tyrants for the Lord"?

"Denying Healthcare to Millions for the Lord" and "Labeling the Free Press an Enemy of the People for the Lord" are just friendly fire casualties in the ultimate battle between Good and Evil.

When my mother was diagnosed with leukemia at the age of 43, the doctor discussed the diagnosis with my father, and together, they decided not to tell my mother, deeming her too emotionally fragile to handle the news.

When a newly assigned nurse met my mother for the first time, she said cheerily, "Oh, you're the leukemia patient." When confronted about his deception, the doctor still refused to give my mother a prognosis, so she asked me to go to the library and report back to her.

The doctor and my father started my mother on chemotherapy without her consent or even her knowledge.

But they were able to form a "righteous" secret combination because their lies and plotting were all for my mother's own good.

She was dead two and a half weeks later.

Far too many Mormons are okay with Trump as the nation's doctor. They just offer their arms for the IVs and do what they're told. After all, Trump's only cleansing the country of people that Jesus would have to eliminate later anyway.

"We thank thee O God for a Second-Anointed One."

Sing along!

With saints like these, who needs sinners?

Ban All Routine Traffic Stops

We must ban all traffic stops that don't involve immediate threats to public safety.

We've all seen the police engage in high-speed car chases in movies and on the news. Such chases are naturally exciting. But so many innocent drivers and pedestrians are killed as a result that some cities have banned car chases entirely.

People do not need to be injured or killed over minor infractions, not the drivers, not the police, and certainly not bystanders.

Likewise, so many routine traffic stops for a broken taillight or driving five miles over the speed limit or having an expired brake tag end up with a police officer shooting an unarmed person, often someone black or brown. And these are drivers who *didn't* flee, who *didn't* pose a threat. But trained police officers are still human beings whose behavior can be influenced by fear and adrenalin. They are people who have grown up in a culture ensuring that even the most open-minded and humane among us have at least some lingering bias. When a life and death decision must be made in a split second, Sunday School lessons on "love thy neighbor" are replaced by the biological imperative to survive.

Are the officers justified in being afraid? Are they overreacting out of bias? We can avoid that emotionally charged debate altogether. More importantly, we can avoid the deadly consequences of both justified and unjustified fear. If police officers are legitimately putting themselves in a life and death situation when stopping a driver for a broken taillight, that traffic stop simply isn't worth the risk. Let the errant driver go, for God's sake. Revenue from issuing tickets doesn't need to drop. Police can record the license plate (like cameras do at stoplights all the time) and mail a ticket to the offender. There's no need for a physical confrontation of any kind, even a mild, orderly one. Not having to spend millions on investigations and settlements, and not having to suffer constant PR nightmares, must surely be worth something as well.

Unless they're stopping a kidnapper or killer or someone suspected of similarly grave crimes, officers should just snap that photo of the license plate and let the driver move on. If we can't justify endangering lives in a car chase over minor violations, then we shouldn't keep endangering them during traffic stops for non-threatening offenses. Such traffic stops are not worth the death of the police officer, the driver, or any passengers in the car. Drug possession or car theft don't warrant the death penalty, after all, even after an arrest and conviction. They certainly don't warrant execution without a trial. If officers are legitimately in danger when pulling people over for any non-violent transgression, then they are risking their lives unnecessarily.

As a child attending my first big tent circus, I remember hearing the announcer say that the trapeze artists were now going to walk across the tightrope without a net. Even at that young age, I thought, "Do they really need to risk killing themselves for this?"

There are times police officers and other first responders need to put their lives on the line. There are times when everyday civilians need to do it, too.

But there's no need for anyone to risk their life just to reprimand someone over a broken taillight. Some officers have even pulled cars over simply because they were driving three miles *under* the speed limit along a corridor frequently used by drug traffickers. If the driver was being so careful not to attract attention, the officers reasoned, he was probably up to no good.

When officers can justify pulling over a car in perfect condition being driven without breaking even the most minor regulation, we have a problem with the status quo.

For the sake of innocent people being killed by the police on a regular basis, we need to stop routine traffic stops that don't involve reckless or intoxicated driving. And even if you're one of those people who don't believe Black Lives Matter, you should *still* want to ban these traffic stops just to protect the people whose lives you *do* think matter.

"We've always done it this way" is no longer a valid rationale for sustaining a policy that inflicts so much unnecessary harm.

Let's ban all routine traffic stops.

Woe unto Them That Are with Child

(published in *Main Street Plaza* on 3 August 2019)

If you were a Jewish couple in 1938 Berlin, would you choose to bring a child into the world?

Groups like Conceivable Future and Birthstrike are among several that have formed recently as more and more young people watching weather reports every day face a question most people in the U.S. have not had to ask themselves before. It's a touchy subject for couples who chose to have children before they fully understood the seriousness of the climate crisis or for those who want to be parents anyway.

Many Christian religions forbid contraception. It was common in my hometown of New Orleans to ask a new acquaintance with six or seven siblings, "I take it you're Catholic?" When my Mormon aunt and uncle lived in South Carolina and people would comment on their large family (three children at the time), they'd smile and say, "We're practically newlyweds. We're just getting started."

Mormons have a particular theology that adds reproductive pressure on couples. They believe they were assigned a quota in the "Pre-existence" committing them to producing a minimum number of bodies for spirits waiting for their chance to come to Earth.

While working as a Mormon missionary in Rome, I became good friends with an Italian sister missionary, Nicla. We wrote regularly after we returned home, and when I came back to Italy to study in Florence, she caught the train from southern Puglia to spend some time with me. A month later, we were engaged.

In Mormon culture, engagements often last only a few weeks, at most a few months. Ours lasted three years. Part of the issue was my decision to wait until I'd graduated college before marrying. Another was to wait until I'd finally managed to stop being gay.

I eventually realized the latter was never going to happen. While it was a moderate loss for me to realize I'd never have any children, it was emotionally devastating for Nicla. We managed to remain friends for the next few decades until her death from breast cancer. She regularly worried she wouldn't be able to marry in time to have children of her own. I remember once quoting Matthew 24:19. "Woe unto them that are with child, and to them that give suck in those days!"

While not the comforting message I'd hoped it would be, I think it's a message every Mormon alive today must consider.

June of 2019 was the hottest June ever recorded by humans. Every day, higher record highs are recorded around the planet. It's hardly even relevant anymore to mention "breaking records," as the new records stand for such a short time. Who knew that temperature readings were only going to have fifteen minutes of fame?

If you knew your child would face Huntington disease or another serious genetic disorder, would you willingly bring that child into the world?

Whatever our religious beliefs, we all have a genetic imperative to reproduce. It's difficult to choose childlessness no matter what extenuating circumstances might suggest it's the better decision.

But wouldn't we be performing a greater service to mankind, to the children already here who face a devastating future, if we devoted the time, energy, and carbon emissions necessary to raise children into addressing the climate crisis instead? If such a decision led to a precipitous decline in human population to a mere one billion, we could always encourage people to start procreating again.

Nicla married in the temple after her childbearing capacity was over and enjoyed an intimate, loving relationship the last years of her life. She died with the comforting belief that when she was resurrected during the Millennium, she'd have an opportunity to bear children then.

Some Mormon politicians, like Senator Mike Lee, claim that the solution to global warming is to have more kids. But that's like saying Paradise, California is blessedly immune from wildfires for the foreseeable future.

The doctrine of many religions allows for the choice of childlessness, or at least the choice of limiting the number of babies we bring into the world. Perhaps a more righteous and caring decision is to work as hard as we can to make life conceivable for all those impatient spirits still waiting for their turn on Earth.

Or at least postpone childbearing until Jesus takes care of it himself.

4 Out of 5 Oligarchs Give Up Their Money and Power When Asked Politely

(published in *LA Progressive* on 12 June 2019)

In a recent survey, 4 out of 5 oligarchs said they were willing to give up their money and power if they were asked politely.

Dubious? You should be. But some activists seem to think otherwise, and that's dangerous for the rest of us.

I received an email the other day from a progressive organization wanting me to sign a petition asking Betsy DeVos to resign. I get these kinds of emails all the time and usually just delete them straight away, but this time, I wrote back. "Can you cite a single example of a person with money and power giving up that money and power because someone else asked them to?" I won't waste my time signing such meaningless documents, and I won't donate my scarce funds to organizations or candidates who think these petitions are useful political acts or clever fundraising strategies.

People with power can't be pressured by the powerless.

In my first relationship, I moved into my partner's house and started paying him rent. From that moment on, whenever we had a disagreement, such as my confusion as to why the rent I paid was higher than the mortgage payment, or whenever I asked for any concession, like being able to use one of the nine rooms in the house for my own belongings, his response was always, "If you don't like it, you can leave."

I didn't see the obvious for quite some time. The following two relationships left me in the same powerless position. But finally, in my current relationship, which has lasted longer than the other three put together, the mortgage is in *my* name. I do listen to my husband's needs and wants, and I feel I make a fair number of concessions. But I'm always aware that *I don't have to*. If my husband chose to leave, it would be inconvenient for me (not to mention sad), but I wouldn't be out in the street, scrambling for a new place to live. Having that little bit of power makes a difference.

Oligarchs, who have a billion times more power and money than most of us ever will, don't have to worry about being inconvenienced when we break up with them. And they won't be sad. The truth is, they won't even notice, the way we don't notice when a spider in our closet crawls out of a shoebox and under the bed. We never knew it was there to begin with.

In any conflict with the rich and powerful, the suffering is all on our side. Reams of evidence prove that empathy and compassion aren't motivating factors for oligarchs.

When employees complain about a new job duty they hadn't signed up for, when they protest not getting the promotion they were promised, when they express unhappiness that their request for a transfer or team assignment has been denied, what they often hear from the boss is, "Take it or leave it."

As leftist voters not represented by the Democratic Party, we are essentially voting in a "right to work" political system that denies us representation or bargaining power. When even powerful unions have difficulty seeing their demands met, a handful of non-union employees signing a petition are likely to be met by their boss's hearty laughter—right before he fires the lot of them. We may be irreplaceable in our own eyes, but the only view that counts is that of the oligarch.

We might garner enough power to bend oppressive oligarchs to our will if we could organize and sustain massive boycotts and strikes that impact them financially. The Montgomery bus boycott worked. Strikers gained weekends off for many workers. Strikes, or the threat of strikes, gained employees the eight-hour workday, paid holidays, and sick leave. However, cornered oligarchs, like cornered animals, routinely lash out in self-defense. Even a brief review of the history of strikes shows that dozens of them don't even bear the name "strike" at all but are called "massacres" instead. Prime Minister Thatcher's oppressive response to striking coal miners severely weakened unions across the UK. Shortly after he took office, President Reagan fired all the air traffic controllers who went on strike in the U.S., and thirty-five years later, workers in all fields still haven't recovered from that blow. Unfortunately, oligarchs have only gained a great deal more power and money since then.

The rich and powerful are able to criminalize many strikes and protests. Even when we're legally allowed to participate in these actions, we face a more immediate and drastic economic impact than the oligarchs we're trying to squeeze. The selection of voting machines and the determination of the boundaries for voting districts are in the hands of oligarchs. It's possible that even a grassroots effort to "get out the vote" will be ineffective at wresting any power back, especially since many Democratic Party leaders are often oligarchs as well.

It may be that our only viable option is "the revolution" that we hear those on the left making vague references to on occasion. There's not a ton of supporting evidence, however, that such an action would resolve much. Only a few years after the French Revolution, Napoleon ruled the country. Hardly a decade passed after the Russian Revolution before almost all socialist ideals were replaced with tyranny.

The best, most effective course of action isn't clear, and we can certainly engage in a healthy debate on the subject. We can make an effort in the courts, at the voting booths, and at town halls. We can march in the streets, boycotting and barricading and striking. We can direct whatever money and power we do possess to candidates and organizations that outline meaningful strategies to help us get through our prolonged constitutional—and existential—crisis. But signing a petition asking Betsy DeVos to "be nice"? We'd have more luck trying to guess the winning numbers for the Powerball.

"Realism" Is What Got Us into This Mess in the First Place

(published in *LA Progressive* on 3 August 2019)

After the Democratic presidential debate on July 30, one of my friends complained about all the "pie in the sky" ideas promoted by the radical candidates. We could never have universal healthcare, he insisted. We could never have tuition-free college. To promote these ideas is to ensure Trump wins again.

It isn't the idealism of unrealistic voters that got Trump elected in 2016. It was the realism of so many voters in the Democratic primaries. The word they use to describe themselves *sounds* wise and mature, but it's a misnomer. Those realists should instead call themselves pessimists.

They are so closed to progressive ideas that they don't realize some form of universal healthcare exists (and has existed for decades) in most other industrialized nations. They don't see that tuition-free college exists (and has for decades) in many other countries. If those are pie in the sky dreams, then lots of other countries are airborne while we're still wallowing in mud pies.

And it's not as if those other countries are Utopias. If they can do it, we certainly can, too.

If fighting for radical changes to address the climate crisis is a pie in the sky dream, pessimists might just as well stop saving for their children's college education right now and spend that money on trips to Disneyland and food festivals instead.

If they honestly believe that slow, incremental change is going to help us in any meaningful way, then they are far from seeing the world "realistically." Even pessimism doesn't describe their philosophy. A better term would be "willfully ignorant." Or perhaps, as offensive a term as it is, "delusional."

But "stubborn" and "obstinate" are accurate terms for them as well. "Arrogant," too, since many of them are so sure their "reasonable" approach will work in a battle against unreasonable fanatics firing scientists at the USDA, against racists blinded by hatred and fear, against faithful sheep brainwashed by right-wing propaganda.

"Realism" is what got us into this mess in the first place. It has no chance of getting us out.

Unless, of course, we correct the definition to reflect reality. If we expect to survive as a nation, as a civilization, then we must immediately make healthcare available to all, so our lives are no longer consumed by the constant struggle to receive care and pay medical bills. Only then will millions of people have the health and emotional energy to face the next battle. We must immediately make college education available to all who want to pursue careers that allow them to support their families. Only then will millions of people have the means and security to handle the rest of the fight. It's the only way we can train enough engineers and meteorologists and biologists to give us a fighting chance to survive the rapidly escalating climate crisis.

That's the reality we face. A world where slow, incremental change was reasonable, was possible, no longer exists.

It's not "moderate" to abandon the chance to survive. It is not "mature and wise" to ignore the science that tells us we have only a handful of years left to make the drastic changes necessary to avoid the collapse of civilization.

It's not "reasonable" to consider climate activists and voters who demand a minimum level of justice "the real problem."

Yes, I'm for realism, too. But let's get real—pie in the sky dreams are not only achievable, they're our only realistic hope.

I Emigrated 2612 Miles Away

When my hometown was devastated by a natural disaster compounded by a man-made one, I fled with one suitcase and ended up relocating over 2600 miles away. Thank God I live in a country large enough that such a radical displacement was still within my nation's borders. For me, this was called "moving."

Seattle welcomed me with open arms when I left New Orleans after Hurricane Katrina. I was "the new guy in apartment B," "the new teller," "the new customer at Washington Mutual." When someone from El Salvador or Guatemala or Ecuador makes a similar move, they're called leeches and freeloaders and dangerous criminals.

But you know, it's only 444 miles from one side of Ecuador to the other, 284 miles from one side of Guatemala to the other, 168 miles from one side of El Salvador to the other. People in some of the poorest countries in our hemisphere don't have the luxury of living in a country as large as the U.S. They often lack the luxury of living in countries free of civil war or other kinds of military and political upheaval.

Worldwide, the U.S. is nowhere near the major destination country for refugees. Smaller nations with fewer resources take in far larger numbers of people fleeing for their lives, certainly per capita but sometimes even in raw numbers.

Let's not pretend there aren't significant differences in resources and options between U.S. refugees and refugees from other countries. How many steps are there from locking up immigrants because they don't deserve freedom to killing such unworthy troublemakers because they don't deserve life? The fact is, when we deport people back to the perilous areas they're fleeing, we're doing just that. At what point does the cost of imprisoning more and more people become so burdensome that we just skip the intermediate steps?

People die in refugee camps. They die in concentration camps. They die when forced to return to countries in turmoil, to countries with few job opportunities and no social safety net.

A white woman in Florida recently berated a Spanish-speaking immigrant, telling her to go back to her own country. The Spanish-speaking woman was from Puerto Rico.

I was lucky. I lived in a country where I could acquire the education and employment necessary for accumulating the savings to afford a plane ticket, a security deposit, and a first month's rent, the savings to buy new clothes and furniture and dishes, the savings to tolerate a month-long break in income. I lived in a country where I had no language barrier to limit success in my new home, where cultural barriers were minimal.

When I immigrated to Seattle with only one suitcase, I carried my birth certificate, my U.S. passport, my checkbook, my credit card, and my resumé.

In short, I wasn't really "lucky." I was privileged.

We expect—no, we demand—that people pull themselves up by their bootstraps. But when we create such a harsh political and economic environment that allows people only this one vital tool, the least we can do is not confiscate it at the border.

Is Recycling Dinosaurs Cost Effective?

The other day, a decal on the side of a car applied next to the gas cap caught my eye. It displayed the traditional symbol for recycling, arrows shaped into a triangle, with the accompanying slogan: Fueled by recycled dinosaurs.

Rape jokes aren't funny. I'd like to say that jokes about raping the environment aren't funny, either, but I admit I laughed. I couldn't help but imagine Elton John repurposing one of his classics into a new hit, "The Triangle of Recycling," for a new Broadway musical, "The Exxon King."

The corporate and political will to aggressively address the climate crisis doesn't exist yet because so many policy influencers profit off the continued destruction of our climate. At what point will fossil fuels stop being cost effective, when corporate profits are offset by billions in crop losses, wildfires, floods, and other disasters? When will our lawmakers finally be forced to stop giving unprecedented tax breaks to the companies causing widespread devastation that taxpayers end up having to pay for as well?

At what point will investment in the capture, storage, and delivery of wind, wave, solar, and thermal energy become cost effective instead?

Have you ever watched the weather forecast before heading off to work? Ever evacuated for a hurricane? Prepared for a blizzard? Reacted to a tornado warning?

Each weather satellite, and there are hundreds, costs between 50 and 400 million dollars, and that doesn't include the 60 million dollars that companies like Space X charge to launch it into orbit. Hundreds of radar systems across the country cost millions more, and meteorologists, as dedicated to the public good as they may be, aren't volunteering their time.

Is that multi-million-dollar investment cost effective? Homes and businesses are still burned by wildfires and inundated by floods. So what's the point of seeing it coming?

Maybe to give us time to pile up sandbags? Open a spillway? Grab our most precious belongings and run for our lives?

Climate crisis deniers dismiss extreme meteorological events as weather, not climate change. But since the only way to measure climate change is through weather, their position is disingenuous.

If fewer people use oil, gas, and coal, shifting instead to wind, solar, and thermal, then oil companies, among the wealthiest corporations on the planet, are perfectly capable of being the ones to develop those renewable energies and the infrastructure to support them. They don't have to lose *any* portion of the market.

But even if they did, aren't conservatives always professing belief in competition and a free market?

When I was growing up, whenever my uncle was driving along a two-way country road and someone tried to pass him, he would speed up so the other driver couldn't pull into the lane ahead of him. When the other driver realized what was happening and tried to slow down and return to the lane behind my uncle, he'd slow down to prevent that as well.

He laughed when he saw a car coming down the road toward the trapped driver in the other lane.

My uncle would not have lost anything if the other driver had passed him or if the other driver had fallen back behind again. Nor did he gain anything by being a prick.

While transitioning from fossil fuels to renewables is not a zero-sum game, where each winner is counterbalanced by a corresponding loser, refusing to make that move is indeed a positive subtraction game where everybody loses.

What sound, reliable business leaders give pep talks to their employees about the glories of lose/lose scenarios?

Iconic American companies like Sears and Woolworth and Kodak and Blockbuster reigned over U.S. commerce for decades. But lack of vision and adaptation to new ideas and innovations has led them each to decline or even go extinct.

There's a reason we call out of touch leaders dinosaurs.

Politicians, voters, and business leaders need to realize that the only win/win approach to combatting climate change is to make drastic modifications immediately. It's too late to save the passenger pigeon and the vaquita porpoise and the northern white rhino. It's too late to save fossil fuel CEOs and the politicians who feed off them. Let's get some fresh DNA in office leading the renewable wave of the only future in which humanity has a chance to evolve.

Cages, Camps, Jails, and Prisons

I was first convicted in a court of law at the age of sixteen.

The District Attorney had walked up to me during breakfast in a cafeteria, staged a crime, and had me arrested. He was desperate to try a case, he apologized.

The first part of the trial went in my favor. I was able to respond to my questioning on the stand with pointed quips that showed I was being framed.

But then we recessed for lunch. And somehow, after we reconvened, the atmosphere in the courtroom changed. Every question seemed more restrictive. I was given parameters for my responses that would no longer permit me to explain the situation as it had actually developed. I'd always been a goody-two-shoes, I thought. How could this be happening to me? I realized with a feeling of dread that I wasn't going to escape disaster.

"I'm innocent!" I concluded.

The verdict was "Guilty," and I was quickly sentenced.

After the trial, a judge who'd been in the courtroom but who hadn't presided over the proceedings came up to me. "I'm so sorry. I saw what happened in the cafeteria, but because I couldn't be impartial, I had to recuse myself."

"If you saw," I countered, "shouldn't you have been on the stand as a witness in my defense?"

Thank God this was only Boys State, I thought to myself. An untucked shirt wasn't going to go on my permanent record. Even if we didn't understand our instructions perfectly during the week-long program to teach high school students more about politics, I had my first inkling that not every convicted felon was truly guilty of the crimes for which they were serving time.

My next conviction came when I was 27. The high priests in my Mormon stake held a Church court. The disciplinary council was, naturally, called a Court of Love. I recognized Orwellian terms after reading *1984* for the first time a few years earlier. I was accused by the stake presidency of having sex with other men. This time I was in fact "guilty" and was subsequently excommunicated. "Please remove your garments," the stake president told me.

I had known this would be the verdict and the first part of my "sentence," so I was not wearing my Mormon underwear that evening and had none to remove. Unlike my sentence at Boys State, this time my "punishment" was freedom, but I still learned something important.

Not all laws determining criminality were just.

And sentencing was more about humiliation than reform.

The United States has the largest prison population per capita in the world. We send far too many innocent men and women to prison daily. Even guilty criminals often spend two or more years in jail waiting for their day in court.

So much for "a speedy trial."

Public defenders have caseloads of 100 clients, 150, 180, or more.

We threaten vulnerable people with such horrific sentences that even innocent people plead guilty to get a "reduced" sentence of a mere seven or eight years.

And yet, if we've made society safer by this "tough on crime" approach, most people in this country don't seem to feel it. We buy more and more guns every day for "self-defense." We put people in cages, in camps, in detention centers. We put people in prison. We deport people with no criminal record because we fear they might one day commit a crime.

We label as criminals fathers trying to protect their children, mothers trying to escape rape.

We put people in jail for fifty years for possessing half an ounce of pot.

Do we really think we're making the world a better place by destroying millions of lives? Our prisons are hardly institutions where inmates learn healthy social skills, where they earn a useful education to pursue gainful careers upon release. Some do, of course, but prison environment ensures that won't be the norm. Even California inmates who risk their lives fighting forest fires for a dollar an hour are often excluded from employment as firefighters after their release.

Americans have a deep, almost addictive need to punish, but we need to start being practical. We have decades and decades of evidence that our prison-industrial complex isn't making our communities healthier.

A friend once asked me, "Do you want to be right or do you want to be happy?" It was a question his sponsor in AA had asked him years earlier.

Sometimes, insisting on getting our way, demanding that others acknowledge our superiority during an argument, guarantees that we *won't* be happy. So what's our real goal?

Punishing more people than any other country in the world hasn't made us happy. If it had, we wouldn't need to "Make America Great Again." We'd already be there. Has putting record numbers of people in for-profit prisons over the last couple of years, separating parents from their children, giving those kids away to strangers, made us happier as a nation? Has it made us feel safer?

There are bad people out there who need to be taken off the streets. But if we already imprison a larger percentage of our population than any other country on Earth, and we still feel we have too many criminals running loose, something is fundamentally flawed about our culture. And that something clearly can't be solved by imprisonment.

Maybe helping people rather than trying as hard as we can to destroy them might produce better results. It seems to work in other countries.

Do we want to be right or do we want to be happy?

God Himself Couldn't Burn This Planet…But Human Denial Can

I hope thousands of people die of heatstroke this summer. I hope another entire town is destroyed by wildfires. I hope a Category 5 hurricane with the highest storm surge ever strikes Miami or Charleston or New York.

I'm okay if this marks me a horrible person. Because I know the only way to save the rest of the country, the rest of the planet, or, really, even a portion of it, is if "the public" finally realizes beyond a shadow of a doubt that the climate crisis is real.

Many Christians believe that God destroyed the world the first time through a global flood and that he'll do it a second time with fire. But it isn't God who's destroying the world. It's spoiled humans whose Heavenly Father seems to let them do whatever they want, no matter how irresponsible.

Humans may eventually behave responsibly, but it's almost always too late for people they've harmed to benefit.

Most communities won't put up a stoplight at a troublesome intersection until a child is run over.

NASA wouldn't fix an acknowledged problem with its O-rings until the space shuttle Challenger exploded shortly after take-off.

Every day on my way to work in south Seattle, I pass dozens and dozens of Boeing 737 MAX planes stored on employee parking lots. Over 500 of the jets are out of commission worldwide as Boeing works to fix a software problem it admits knowing about over a year before the first of two crashes that killed 346 people. Even the first crash wasn't enough to spur them to address the problem.

Our knee-jerk reaction is to think that city councils and NASA and Boeing are run by terrible people, but really their behavior is normal. As humans, we simply don't like to believe the situations we find ourselves in are bad until we are forced to face them in undeniable ways.

Unfortunately, that means we must accept the deaths of thousands from heat stroke, the obliteration of entire towns, the loss of billions of dollars from storm and drought damage, before we'll do what must be done.

It would be far cheaper and less deadly to deal with problems up front, but humans are gamblers by nature, even though we all know the house always wins. Sometimes, we stop placing bets before we're bankrupt, and sometimes, we don't.

I'm not sure there's a way to skip a step in this process of denial and get right to the problem-solving part.

Humans will have no choice but to address the climate crisis on a local, national, and global level. The science is not debatable. It's the psychology that is.

How much are we willing to lose before we as a species are collectively ready to accept what must be done?

Promoters of the White Star Line boasted in 1912 that the *Titanic* was so well built "even God himself couldn't sink this ship." And God *didn't* sink that ship. Arrogant men who thought they were more powerful than Nature sunk that ship.

If I'm an ass for wanting our nation's voters to wake up, what does it make those who work actively to keep us in denial until all five hundred 737 MAX planes plummet to the earth? Is it okay to encourage people to accept even just twenty more crashes?

The temperature reached a record 114 degrees F in France in June of 2019. It reached an all-time high of 90 in Anchorage, Alaska a few days later.

The hottest two months of the summer are still ahead of us.

I hope your grandma dies of heat stroke. I hope your cousin's hometown is destroyed by wildfires. I hope a Category 5 strikes New York while you're there on a business trip.

Not even the most radical eco-activists would try to "help" by deliberately creating problems, but surely we must be aware that foreign or domestic terrorists have access to matches. At least a few have access to surface-to-air missiles that could be used to knock out the power grid of a major city during the height of a heatwave. Or damage our water infrastructure.

The dangers are real, with or without additional malice. One way or another, Grandma's on her way out.

Maybe we can just catch a plane to someplace cool and deny reality a bit longer. I hear the melting glaciers of Greenland are nice this time of year.

It's Not Business, It's Personal

We've all seen movies about the Mafiosi, where a mob boss will have a former "friend" executed. He sometimes apologizes for the imminent murder, saying, "It's not personal, it's business." But we all realize that it *is* personal—it's the guy's goddamn life, after all—and we understand instantly that even if what the mob boss was saying were true, killing someone purely for business reasons is hardly a point in the murderer's favor.

When we ask our religious friends how they can support Trump despite all his horrific behavior toward the poor, to those seeking asylum, to everyday workers, to farmers, to women, to those suffering in almost any way both in the U.S. and around the world, they often say, "Well, I don't approve of him *personally*, but he's good for business."

When the soul of the religious right is indistinguishable from the heart of a mob boss, Trump isn't the only person we need to worry about.

Bullet Points

(previously published in *Who Invited You to the Orgy?*)

- 52% of Americans feel that more guns make us less safe

- 60% of Americans favor stricter gun laws

- 73% of Americans think that the U.S. isn't doing enough to address gun violence

- 93% of Americans support background checks for all gun buyers

When I asked a coworker once what some of her hobbies were, she said, "I like to watch videos online of people dying. You know, videos taken at the scene of car accidents, people jumping off bridges, things like that."

I was appalled. What kind of person would actively seek out such images? But after the massacre at two mosques in New Zealand, I realized it might be more psychologically damaging *not* to watch people dying. On the one hand, I appreciate that limiting the "fame" of murderers and terrorists is a good thing. And I can't begin to imagine how awful it would be for relatives and friends of those killed in the attack to see even a moment of the footage that monster filmed as he slaughtered their loved ones.

But at a certain point, protecting viewers lets lawmakers, gun manufacturers, the NRA, and even ourselves off the hook. Those deaths remain theoretical and abstract. We hear the numbers of people killed, but they remain numbers for most of us, not people. We can't understand the full horror we support because the "sensibilities" we're "protecting" are our own.

I remember feeling disturbed during the second Bush administration when news organizations were no longer allowed to film caskets filled with dead soldiers from the Iraq war being carried off of planes. Whatever respect such censorship might show the families who'd lost a son or husband or father or mother or sister or daughter, the end result was that the majority of Americans never saw the consequences of entering that unjustified war.

In the first days after the attack on the World Trade Center, news programs repeatedly aired footage of people jumping out of the burning building to their deaths. The scenes were horrific. I can still see those people in my mind all these years later. Because people matter to our psyches more than buildings or airplanes ever will.

When I watched Michael Moore's "Fahrenheit 11/9," I was shocked to see cell phone video taken by students as the Parkland shooter gunned down their classmates and teachers. There's a fine line between exploitation and honesty, and Moore stayed on the right side of that line. But that massacre hit me with much greater force when I *saw* it than it did when I *heard* about it, and it hit me pretty heavily even then.

Seeing is believing.

Hearing about children in cages is abstract. Seeing them in cages induces a visceral reaction. Reading about a school on lockdown because of a fake bomb threat can be shrugged off in the cacophony of bad news we hear every day. But seeing photos of a 7-year-old's forearm where the girl had written "Love Mom and Dad" with a purple marker just in case she got killed is heartrending. Reading a book about the tsunami following the 1883 eruption of Krakatoa is interesting. Watching video of the 2004 Indian Ocean tsunami makes the horror of such an event real.

The story of the Andes plane crash survivors is fascinating on its own. But the fact that the survivors took photos during their 72-day ordeal makes it unforgettable. President John F. Kennedy's assassination would have made an impact under any circumstances, but because the murder was filmed, and because that film has been aired hundreds of times over the last fifty-five years, we will all remember how a promising life and career can end instantly at the pull of a trigger. Even now, because these words are attached to a visual memory in our brains, we can see Jackie leaping out of her seat and crawling across the trunk of the car to grab part of her husband's skull.

If a news organization reports that a police officer shot and killed a suspect in self-defense, many of us are willing to take the officer's word. But when we see with our own eyes a video of an officer shooting an unarmed Black man in the back, or shooting an unarmed Black man lying on the floor with his hands up, while we hear that man begging "Please don't kill me" as the officer aims and fires, we *know* in the deepest level of our souls that we've just witnessed the deplorable reality of structural racism.

Seeing the truth about gun violence, no matter who is committing it, is essential if we are to realize our right "to life, liberty, and the pursuit of happiness."

Those opposed to showing these ghastly images claim that doing so will make survivors, and the loved ones of those killed, experience their grief again and again. That may be, but grieving people don't own our history and legislation and morality. The rest of us have a right to know what we're up against so we can act accordingly.

Seeing is understanding.

Critics claim that seeing this violence and blood and gore on a regular basis will desensitize viewers. That may be true as well, but what good has all our sensitivity gotten us? Some thoughts and prayers? The only chance we have to accomplish the difficult changes necessary is if we *cannot* avoid the abominations we're told we shouldn't politicize.

News anchors can announce "trigger warnings" right before going to commercial alerting viewers that these images will be aired immediately after the break. Or we can make the images available online only to those who deliberately click on a link. I'm not proposing, after all, that we reenact "A Clockwork Orange."

If I say Kent State 1970, what image comes to mind?

How about Tiananmen Square?

Or the Black woman in Baton Rouge standing calm and serene in a sundress as police in riot gear descend upon her?

Some historians say that the photo of the "napalm girl" in Vietnam helped change the course of the war.

Emmett Till's mother insisted on an open casket for her son who'd been tortured and murdered by a white mob. She wanted people to *see* what those savages did to him. Every one of us who has seen that photo, even all these years later, is sickened by the sight—except those so filled with hatred and bigotry they can no longer experience empathy or compassion.

What happened in Sandy Hook was so nightmarish that even without seeing photos of six-year-olds on the floor with their brains splattered across the tiles, we still *almost* generated enough indignation to change gun laws. Would we have been able to cross that threshold if we'd actually seen those pictures?

Seeing motivates us.

Yes, it's possible terrorists or psychopaths will get a kick out of seeing the carnage, but haters and murderers and politicians whose pockets are lined with money from the NRA aren't going to be any more helpful if we respectfully sensor the atrocities they support. The killings simply continue unabated. The next Las Vegas concert massacre, the next Pittsburgh synagogue shooting, the next Aurora movie theater slaughter comes along anyway.

And is quickly forgotten. Because we have no haunting images seared into our minds.

We cannot reduce suffering if we can't even bear to see it. We don't need to show every single photo and every single video, but we must show *some* of them. For these gun deaths to matter, they must become more than bullet points in a rhetorical discussion. Words are essential, but it will take images as well to pierce us in the deeply primal way necessary to move us to action.

Leaders Should Lead, Not Block
Forward Movement

Leaders should help people move forward, not crush them back.

When I signed up for my first Organic Chemistry course, I was a little intimidated. For years, I'd heard horror stories about how difficult the subject was. So I was surprised on my first day of class to hear my professor say something to the effect of, "Most of you need this course to get into medical school, so I'm going to make sure you don't get an A. You heard this was hard? You have no idea. You're going to regret taking this class."

I didn't regret it. I dropped it the moment I left that day. I remembered Maya Angelou's advice, "When someone shows you who they are, believe them the first time."

I signed up for Organic Chemistry with another professor and enjoyed a course that turned out to be fun and exciting. Organic Chemistry wasn't hard—it was a game, a puzzle. I made an A in both Organic Chemistry I and II.

I didn't make it into med school, but it wasn't Organic Chemistry that kept me back.

Leaders should help those they're leading be the best they can be, not work to make sure they're the worst. There's a reason leaders are not called crushers.

After I came out, I joined the New Orleans Gay Men's Chorus. One year, the New Orleans Opera chorus asked us to join them in a production of *Aida*. They wanted to make a spectacular production, so we were to add bodies on stage as the priests' chorus. This was going to be a lot of fun.

Only it wasn't. The director was an unpleasant SOB who criticized us every few minutes. We were no good. We were ruining his production. He thought he should probably just dump us and do without our voices. At one point, he said, "You don't even follow me. What am I even here for? Follow me!"

He instructed us to start a certain section over, and there was a point where we were all supposed to join in loudly, but he didn't signal us, so we didn't. The director then shouted, "You guys can't even read music! Why didn't you come in when you were supposed to?"

He'd set us up to fail. He *wanted* us to fail more than he wanted us to succeed.

We went on to sing in both performances of *Aida*, and once we were on stage in front of a huge audience, we had a good time anyway because the guy had to shut up and do his job. Were we good? Were we bad? I don't know. What I do know is we would probably have sung better if we'd had a leader who wanted to help us move forward rather than prove his superiority by crushing us.

I see this same dynamic over and over in the arts, but I see it elsewhere, too. Is it even possible *not* to see this in the world of politics?

As Speaker of the House, Nancy Pelosi doesn't "lead" as much as she crushes. She's done all she can to squash "the squad" of four first-year representatives trying to do their job. She's so intent on the act of crushing that she hasn't even noticed the world has changed, that her policy positions are out of touch with millions of voters, that in the midst of a constitutional crisis and an even more desperate climate crisis, the time for slow, moderate change has come and gone.

A friend taught me long ago to watch people carefully who we're considering taking into our lives. Watch how they treat wait staff, he said, or other service personnel, anyone "lower" on the social scale, because the worst way they treat anyone else is the way they'll eventually treat you.

We're often faced with determining how sincere candidates are who might have good policy ideas and platforms. We can look at their past actions to help us clarify their true character. Are they for Medicare for All now but in the past have sided with pharmaceutical companies? We'd better take that into consideration. We can also see how they interact with other candidates, with their prospective constituents, with reporters.

Let's choose carefully in the upcoming primaries and elections. A decent follower is far better than a bad leader. But whatever we do, let's make sure not to elect crushers.

Organic Water, Clean Natural Gas, and Giftwrapped Garbage

A television commercial I saw the other day displayed a bottle labeled "Organic Water." Naturally, this gave me pause, as by definition, organic compounds must contain at least one carbon molecule. And there's no C in H_2O.

Looking more closely, I realized that in this case, "Organic" was part of the branding, not a description of the water itself. Still, it was hard not to feel misled. Organic water *sounds* healthy.

Greta Thunberg, the young Swedish climate activist, said that one of our biggest obstacles in addressing the climate crisis is that too many of us might be deceived by the spin oil and gas companies put on their "efforts" to limit carbon emissions. A couple of years ago, some fossil fuel corporations began airing commercials touting "clean" natural gas. More spin soon followed.

Burning fossil fuels is never clean, and since so much of the natural gas we use is extracted via fracking, we must also consider the millions of gallons of water permanently contaminated each day by the process.

There's no such thing as clean coal, either.

We've all heard the story about an enterprising man frustrated by a long garbage strike who put his household refuse in a box every day, giftwrapped it, and then slapped a bow on top. He would place the "gift" in the back seat of his car, park at a shopping center, and leave the car door unlocked. When he would return to his car later, he would happily discover that his garbage was now someone else's problem.

While the story is likely apocryphal, this is essentially the same strategy used by fossil fuel corporations, only they are getting paid to foist their garbage on us. Over 550 toxic coal ash ponds are some of the permanent gifts that residents near coal mines are privileged to enjoy.

Climate scientists keep pointing out that while global warming will increase rainfall in some areas, often that extra rain will descend in downpours so heavy they'll cause catastrophic flooding. Other areas will see significantly less rain. The Sahara, we should remember, was once a large, verdant region of Africa until the last period of rapid climate change.

A recent study in *Nature Geoscience* reveals that almost 150 million trees were killed in California between December of 2011 and March of 2019 as a result of drought combined with higher temperatures. While that is a staggering number, we should realize it isn't a *final* number. More droughts and increasingly higher temperatures, both consequences of accelerating climate change, plus the resultant increase in wildfires every year, will keep killing more and more trees. The number won't stop at 150 million. Or 200 million. Or 250 million.

In *The Day after Tomorrow*, the character played by Dennis Quaid tells a group of politicians that an iceberg the size of

Rhode Island just broke off an ice sheet. Currently, in Antarctica, the Thwaites ice sheet, the size of Florida, is collapsing. That is in addition to the 35 gigatons of ice a year we've lost between 2009 and 2017.

But we don't have to wait for cataclysmic sea level rise before we start experiencing serious water crises. Many of those toxic coal ash ponds gifted to us by fossil fuel companies overflowed during Hurricane Florence's assault on the Carolinas in 2018. Over fifty lagoons filled with pig waste overflowed as well.

I'm not sure we *want* organic water.

The Cuyahoga River in Ohio has caught fire several times from industrial debris and oil slicks in its waters.

Tap water near many fracking sites is easily ignitable.

In 1982, my first partner's grandmother heard an explosion near her home in Kenner, Louisiana. She ran outside into a heavy downpour, terrified to see the rain all about her ablaze. She didn't realize a plane had just crashed. She thought she was witnessing the end of the world.

It's essentially what we are all witnessing today. Oh, there will certainly be species that survive the current mass extinction event. We might even be among them.

In books and movies about nuclear war, there are always human survivors. But few of them ever seem very happy. We face a similarly hellish future across much of our planet if we don't begin taking drastic action now.

We can't giftwrap trillions of gallons of contaminated water.

We can't call water organic just because it contains carbon molecules from fossil fuels.

We can't irrigate our drought-stricken agricultural regions with water crammed full of lethal chemicals.

But if we're lucky, we can have our children's bodies treated with organic embalming fluids before we dig a hole in the hard-baked ground to hide their coffins.

Socialists Are Crybabies

A former missionary companion of mine on Facebook reposted a long rant by a young, privileged conservative. In her essay, "My Generation Is Bling to the Prosperity Around Us," published by the Foundation for Economic Education, Alyssa Ahlgren points out how spoiled socialist crybabies are who want to "fix" the "so-called injustices" caused by capitalism.

As she explains how lucky even the poorest Americans are, how our poverty level is 31 times that of the global average, how "ungrateful" lefty Democratic bellyachers are, I was fascinated by the process by which she experiences her epiphany.

While sitting in a coffeeshop, she browses the news on her phone. Then she looks around at all the happy, wealthy people around her, those working on computers, driving cars past the shop, ordering food. What kind of candy-ass wimps bitch in the midst of all this abundance?

My former missionary colleague, I might point out, grew up in Pebble Beach, one of the richest neighborhoods in California. He's a physician now. He recently posted about a trip to Paris which afforded his family the opportunity to enjoy Disneyworld there, the "main focus" of the trip.

Good for him. That sounds fun. But it's disingenuous to pretend all Americans enjoy the same level of privilege. Alyssa is using the word "privileged" to acknowledge her own but repurposing the word to mean something completely different when applied to the poor. The technique would be called equivocation if she were doing it consciously, but I get the sense she's simply clueless.

There are the privileged rich and the privileged poor. Her equivocation allows her to persuade the rich that their privilege is the same as the privilege an elderly woman has dying of heat stroke in her unairconditioned apartment. Sure, the old woman is privileged to have an apartment, but not privileged enough to make the place survivable. I don't think Ahlgren or my FB friend have that problem.

The woman in the coffeeshop is educated enough to pursue an MBA but not enough to understand that socialism is an economic system, not a form of government. True socialism demands a full democracy.

The privileged coffee drinker talks of the millions killed under the tyranny of "socialism" that was actually communism but seems to have no concept that our glorious capitalist society (which is a republic, not a democracy) has murdered people, too. Are Native Americans and blacks the privileged heroes she is referring to when she says socialists are going to destroy "what millions of people have died to achieve"? She seems to have no concept that the U.S. imprisons a larger percentage of our own population than either modern China or the former Soviet Union during its infamous gulag period. It hasn't even occurred to her that these might be counterarguments. These points haven't entered her mind to be considered and tossed out in the first place. They simply don't warrant that much thought.

I'd like to tell my former missionary companion, the physician, that my sister is a nurse whose employer doesn't provide health insurance. She's sixty and hasn't gone to the doctor in years. Mind you, she's a conservative, too. She's not bitching about capitalism. I just think she should.

I don't sit at coffeeshops in my neighborhood reflecting on how stupid and selfish the poor people around me are, or even about how stupid and selfish the rich are. Mostly because I can't afford to go to a coffeeshop. I can't even afford a cell phone. When I catch the first of three buses to get to work, I watch as destitute people along the route beg the driver for a free ride. Some drivers let them board. Others don't. As a result, some of these wannabe passengers get to their jobs on time and some don't.

It's not easy to support a family on minimum wage, even if you have the privilege to work a few hours of overtime each week. It's even harder when so many employers won't hire you full-time in the first place, so they can avoid giving you any benefits.

The ranting conservative sipping her coffee went on to point out how all those people bitching about capitalism can simply turn on their computer, order a blender on Amazon, and have it delivered to their door the next day.

Is this her equivalent to Herbert Hoover's "a chicken in every pot and a car in every garage"?

The privileged woman continued her Facebook rant by pointing out how crybabies don't even recognize the privilege we have "to associate with whom we choose." I have to wonder how many political protests she's participated in. A police officer, commenting on an 84-year-old woman who'd been pepper-sprayed at a peaceful protest, said, "What did she expect?" It's easy to feel the joy of American freedom if YOU have it, but this woman in the coffee shop, and my friend who reposted her wise reflections, have "become completely blind" to their privilege.

That's me repurposing her accusation that the poor don't realize how good they have it.

I can concede that the sleeping bag I saw a homeless man lying in on my way to work the other day did seem to be of reasonably high quality. When the coffee drinker writes that "virtually no one in the United States is considered poor by global standards," does she really think that 550,000 homeless people is truly a number so close to zero?

The privileged woman then went on to quote Alexandria Ocasio-Cortez, who'd said the most "factually illiterate thing" the woman had ever heard, that "an entire generation...never saw American prosperity."

The privileged woman is right. OF COURSE we've all seen prosperity. We simply haven't experienced it very much. There's a difference between standing on the sidewalk watching through a window as a woman on her phone sips $5 coffee while eating a $5 scone and actually enjoying any of those privileges ourselves.

The privileged woman concludes that the reason stupid Americans want socialism is that we've "ONLY" seen prosperity. We've never been through a depression or a world war. We don't know what the world is really like for people who aren't caught in the "trap of entitlement."

She then goes on to finish her cup of expensive coffee. If she runs to the bathroom before leaving, does she realize there are still places in every state where people are too poor to have indoor plumbing? Her privileged plumbing also provides her with fresh drinking water. Those sissies in Flint don't realize how good she has it.

I wonder if she has any friends or family "entitled" enough to join the military and have their legs blown off because signing up was the only viable employment opportunity available to them.

I am privileged enough to own a computer. I have a roof over my head. I even have health insurance. I'm grateful to be nowhere near the bottom of the pile.

But many of the privileged poor in America can't afford their insulin. Of course, I can hear the young woman's response to that—only someone living on rice and pasta and potatoes and Ramen noodles is privileged enough to develop diabetes. There are people all over the world who would kill for unhealthy food.

My husband is 66 and can't afford his premium for supplemental insurance. Medicare doesn't cover everything.

I expect that's something the privileged woman in the coffeeshop looking at all the privileged people in her privileged neighborhood doesn't even know.

Are socialists crybabies? Perhaps we are. Babies cry when they're hungry. They cry when they're ignored.

And they cry when they're spanked for crying.

The privileged rich are disgusted by those complaining about their privileged poverty. I think it's fine if the privileged rich want to wallow in their privilege. Why shouldn't they? I certainly enjoy even the lower level of privilege I have and am glad to have every bit of it.

But let's call a golf ball a golf ball. Those fighting "to fix the injustices of capitalism" aren't deluded. We know exactly what side the scone is buttered on.

Climate Crisis Threatens the Mormon Church

(published in *Main Street Plaza* on 12 August 2019)

While the devastating effects of the climate crisis will help fulfill prophecies about the terrors of the "last days," that's about the only benefit the Mormon Church will receive from them. Virtually every other effect will weaken the Church.

Members of The Church of Jesus Christ of Latter-day Saints often feel they are given special protection by Heavenly Father, despite scriptures claiming God is "no respecter of persons." In almost every account of natural disaster, we hear about how "the chapel was miraculously spared," "no missionary was harmed," or some other such claim. The truth, though, is that Mormons are increasingly impacted by the effects of worldwide climate crisis, both at home and abroad.

Scientists have determined that as global temperatures rise, so does sea level. Storms become more frequent, and because upper level steering currents are disrupted by climate change, even small storms can linger over an area and cause widespread devastation. In 2017, flooding impacted roughly 1400 Peruvian Latter-day Saints.

That same year, Hurricane Harvey dumped over five feet of rain and flooded six LDS meetinghouses in the Houston area, causing minor damage to another twenty. 800 homes of church members were damaged, with 2800 members displaced. Even the Houston temple was flooded.

In 2018, Hurricane Florence in the Carolinas flooded the homes of 20 members. Cyclone Gita seriously damaged a ward meetinghouse in Tonga as well as the Liahona high school there. Over in Samoa and American Samoa, Gita flooded the LDS Service Center and damaged the stake center in Pago Pago.

Just a few years earlier, Typhoon Haiyan destroyed the homes of hundreds of church members. According to the Deseret News, "In one Mormon congregation alone, 95 percent of the members saw their homes destroyed. Scores had lost family members, many carried out to sea with the current, never to return."

At least two ward meetinghouses were destroyed by Hurricane Katrina in 2005. Many displaced members in Louisiana and Mississippi moved out of the area permanently.

In 2016, an LDS stake center in Denham Springs, Louisiana was submerged when a storm stalled over the Baton Rouge area for days.

In 2008, Nauvoo was threatened by floods in the American Midwest. In 2019, the town was flooded. The Mormon Bridge connecting Nebraska and Iowa was washed away.

Extreme weather events caused by global warming are becoming more common around the world. They affect everyone, and since Mormons are part of "everyone," they affect members of the Church as well. Even those who don't lose their homes (or their lives) are impacted when FEMA and other government agencies use billions in taxpayer dollars to address disaster after disaster after disaster.

In 2017, members of the Mormon Church lost 150 homes in 16 California wildfires in Santa Rosa, Napa, Ukiah, Auburn, and Coffey Park. A mission home, a meetinghouse, and an Institute building were threatened. They survived the fires that year, but the Church will need to deal with more and more losses as wildfires in the west worsen in the coming years.

In 2018, 20 member families lost homes in the Carr fire near Redding, California. One can look up stark images of wildfires burning behind the Payson temple in Utah.

And who can forget the devastation wreaked upon members in Paradise that year? Two meetinghouses burned to the ground, the fire so intense that a metal beam supporting the roof of one of them melted. Almost every member in town, over 60 families, lost their homes.

These are no longer isolated incidents. This is the future of life on Earth as the climate crisis worsens and we continue to refuse addressing it.

It bears remembering that all these disasters also impact the missionaries serving there at the time and disrupt missionary work in the area for years afterward.

Of course, nothing is *all* bad. Even climate crisis has a silver lining for Mormons. Temple work, in those temples that survive, will receive a boost, given the increased opportunity to perform baptisms for the dead.

Kinda gives "Jesus wants me for a sunbeam" a rather different meaning, doesn't it?

De-escalation Is More Feasible Than Eliminating Bias

De-escalation classes at all levels are a more effective strategy for reducing unjustified police shootings than calling officers out for their racism.

A few days ago, I shared a video on Facebook from Occupy Democrats showing an encounter between a white police officer and a black college student that escalated quickly into a life and death situation.

Like many Americans, I'm tired of seeing these encounters spiral out of control, resulting in the deaths of unarmed men, women, and children who have not broken a single law.

Part of the problem, though, is that even lots of folks on the left keep blaming the victims. After I posted the video, a good friend of mine, a progressive, humane man who has spent his life serving others, sent me an email explaining why he thought the problem in this case was created by the black student, not the white officer. The student, he said, was being an ass.

My immediate reaction was to wonder how many times in the past I was guilty of the same attitude, how many times even now my subconscious biases affect my opinions and actions. I, too, was ambivalent about the man in the video. But he was picking up trash, which is not particularly threatening. Extremely few people do that just before robbing a place.

And the officer repeatedly saying he can shoot the guy because he's holding a trash picker makes the officer a far bigger threat to public safety. But even if we concede the student was the most awful asshole in the world, it isn't a crime to be obnoxious. Threatening to kill imperfect people should be.

White dominant culture has programmed us to care too much about proper (white) etiquette. I feel similar emotions when I see black people "misbehaving" on the bus or in the grocery store. I may judge myself for my reaction, but that self-judgment always comes *after* my immediate judgment of the "inappropriate" behavior I've just witnessed. The problem is that cultural attitudes toward etiquette contribute to the anger that escalates these encounters. Police officers are *angry* that people aren't following the "right" cultural norms. And it's virtually impossible in the heat of the moment to ignore learned culture that feels instinctive to us.

We need de-escalation training at all levels of society. We must provide it in our elementary schools, our middle schools, our high schools, our community colleges, our universities. It's a class all of us are going to need to participate in over and over. We need de-escalation training in the workplace as well. Even small businesses should be able to purchase a DVD their employees can watch. But we don't have to put the onus on employers. De-escalation courses can be taught in community centers across the country.

They'd be great along with mandatory courses on racism, sexism, and bias of all kinds.

We will all benefit from de-escalation training, even if we never encounter a police officer with a trigger finger and a short temper. Proficiency at de-escalation will help us on those days we need to deal with an unhelpful customer service rep. If we're the customer service rep ourselves, it would help us with practically every interaction we conduct during our entire workday. Every one of us can use de-escalation techniques to solve problems with our coworkers and our bosses. We need the training to resolve issues with our neighbors. With our students. With our teachers. With people on the bus. With other drivers on the road.

What marital relationship wouldn't benefit if we all learned de-escalation techniques before saying, "I do"? What kind of impact would such training have on our relationships with our parents or our children or our in-laws?

White folks need to accept that their dismissal of the injustices people of color face because they aren't behaving "politely" is part of the problem. That doesn't make us terrible people. It just means we need to force ourselves to learn and grow and keep trying to become a little less racist every day.

Maybe that college student with the bad attitude does need to behave better. But so do we white folks. Dismissing the harassment and killing of blacks or anyone else for not having good etiquette is bad behavior, bad behavior we must stop.

De-escalation training will help us get past our "triggers," both emotional and literal, and reduce the number of senseless police shootings.

With Friends Like These: The Liberal Media's Attack on Progressive Policies

(published in *LA Progressive* on 9 June 2019)

Most of my liberal friends watch MSNBC religiously. Those slightly less liberal watch CNN or other "leftist" news sources. I used to watch MSNBC every night as well. But I learned early in the 2016 election cycle that my favorite news organization was biased against progressive values. I still watch occasionally, but on June 3 of this year, I saw a few minutes on Brian Williams's show that made me feel I was watching Fox News from an alternate universe.

I finally understand what alt right means.

Williams showed two brief clips of lesser-known Democratic candidates for president, John Hickenlooper of Colorado and John Delaney of Maryland. Speaking at a state convention in California, Hickenlooper told those in attendance, "Socialism is not the answer." The crowd booed him loudly for a sustained period. When Delaney told them, "Medicare for All may sound good, but it is actually not good policy nor is it good politics," he also received long, loud boos from the audience.

But it was what happened next that shocked me. Rather than report on the growing number of Democrats in every state who want the Party to move to the left, rather than report on the growing number of Democrats who are leaving the Party altogether because it *won't* move to the left, rather than report on an effective way to move forward, Brian Williams asked Rick Wilson, a Republican strategist, for his analysis.

After mocking progressive Democrats in California as the "wokest of the woke," Wilson went on to give his expert opinion that Democrats in California "give way to all their impulses. They really don't care if these things play politically across the nation." A progressive agenda was completely unviable.

Williams then turned to another guest to ask her opinion but prefaced his question with his conclusion: "He is so right."

To be fair, I was already primed to take offense, after Williams earlier in the show described a protester at Kamala Harris's rally as a "very entitled animal rights activist." Is it just me, or does that sound dismissive of people who care about stopping the abuse of animals? What would an unentitled animal rights activist look like, and why doesn't Williams report on any of their work?

The overall message from *The 11ᵗʰ Hour*, which came through loud and clear, is that "liberals" are out of touch, extreme, selfish, and delusional. Most importantly, they are going to ruin everything for all the sane, normal Democrats. You know, people like George Will.

In 2015, Rachel Maddow interviewed Debbie Wasserman Schultz at the start of the presidential election cycle. When Wasserman Schultz stated that the DNC was going to make Hillary Clinton the nominee, even Rachel recoiled onscreen at the blatantly unethical declaration. What voters wanted was never going to be important to Wasserman Schultz and the DNC. The decision had already been made before the primaries even began.

Melissa Harris-Perry resigned/was fired from her successful morning show on MSNBC not long after because the network wanted her, she said, "to cover politics in the narrowest sense."

As I continued to watch MSNBC through the rest of that election cycle, it seemed as if every show, all morning, all afternoon, all evening, covered Trump for roughly forty-five minutes of each hour. Clinton might be covered for thirteen minutes, Sanders for one if he was lucky, and some other candidate or story might be covered briefly on occasion. The media that liberals trusted elevated Trump by wasting enormous amounts of time on him day after day after day. They helped Trump win every bit as much as the Russians or anyone else.

In the years since, most liberal media outlets haven't covered the fight for Net Neutrality. They don't report on the growing number of socialists and Democratic Socialists. They don't report on the steadily increasing support for universal healthcare or tuition-free college or re-enfranchisement of ex-felons or the desperate need to ban all new fracking and pipelines. There is almost no reporting on efforts to eliminate the Electoral College, no stories on the support for guaranteed childcare, on the successes that dozens of other nations have achieved on these and other progressive issues.

They certainly don't offer editorial support when they do. Instead, they actively work to discredit such "crackpot" ideas.

The liberal media are anything but. They and most other "left-leaning" news sources are not reporting. They are spinning.

What's amazing is that despite their massive power to influence, these iconic news outlets are losing countless voters to the far left anyway. Millions of us can see the manipulation and distortion of the issues and candidates.

Being "realistic" about limited access to healthcare isn't progressive. Being "practical" on prison reform isn't progressive. Being "patient" on climate change isn't progressive.

We can only be told for so long that our political future will be bright and sunny if we just know our place and keep in line, while we sit looking out our windows at the heavy rain flooding the streets, trapping us in front of our screens.

Their Eyes Were Watching…a Sit-Com

My husband won't watch *Schindler's List*. One of our friends won't watch *Upstairs Inferno*. A coworker of mine turns the channel if an SPCA commercial comes on. These are good people, kind and generous. But the defense they and others like them use—"I'm too sensitive. I can't watch things like that"—is a fault that must be overcome.

I mentioned to a friend that there was a scene in Michael Moore's documentary *Fahrenheit 11/9* incorporating cell phone video from a student during the Parkland shooting. He said he'd never watch that film, that he couldn't stomach such horrors.

But I wonder. If we refuse to see, are we still moved to action? Do we vote for candidates who want to pass common sense gun regulations? Do we research the best organizations to feed and educate suffering children in other countries, and then actually get around to donating? Do we talk to our friends and family about these issues?

Being sensitive isn't terribly useful if it doesn't lead to positive action.

One of my coworkers turns the channel any time the news shows a video of immigrant children crowded into cages. "I can't bear to watch those poor children."

Another friend "opted out" of watching *The Hate U Give* with me. "It's too tense. It's too true-to-life."

"Those are exactly the reasons we need to see it," I told him.

He chose to do something else.

But "out of sight, out of mind" is an accurate proverb. Once we choose not to face the images, we often move on to other subjects altogether.

I asked a colleague how many people like us she thought were still working in any meaningful way to get help for Puerto Rico, still devastated by Hurricane Maria.

"Oh, I forgot all about that," she said.

Exactly.

Of course, this lack of awareness or action isn't always the case. My husband participates in counter-protests against neo-Nazis regularly, volunteering as security to help protect the counter-protesters from violence. He also volunteered this last Pride to help protect the participants in Seattle's Trans Pride parade. He's been pepper sprayed and pushed about. My husband isn't living in a protective bubble of Hallmark movies just because he won't watch *Guilty Until Proven Guilty*.

But I fear too many of us are. I've heard friends say we'll become desensitized if we watch too much suffering and begin to feel less need to act. I wonder, though, if that's not just rationalizing our choice to ignore various crises "for now."

While we have to recognize our personal limitations and work within them, when a given limitation is *too* limiting, we need to challenge ourselves to do better.

I feel stupid and embarrassed at rallies when leaders ask the protesters to chant slogans. I'm quiet and reserved by nature. I feel silly shouting, raising my arms, and shaking my fist in the air. But since subdued protesting is not terribly effective, I've found ways to get around that. I can make a sign that voices my feelings, hopefully in a clever way. My "voice" then still gets heard.

Another of my workarounds is to reframe the situation in my mind. When I'm at a protest, I'm no longer "me" but an actor in a public performance. "I'm" not the person shouting slogans. The character I'm portraying is. And it's a show the community needs to see.

But when news crews won't report on the protest, or politicians refuse to watch, we're back where we started.

He who has eyes to see, let him see.

Religious adherents who refuse to see their religious institution's problematic history are not moved to insist their leaders do better.

Conservatives who refuse to tune in to anything other than Fox News are not moved to demand Republican politicians act more humanely.

Liberals who refuse to watch international news are not moved to push for necessary policy changes around the globe.

If *we* won't look at things that make us uncomfortable, we can't expect others to do so, either.

Yet if we can find ways to make ourselves look, we'll gain insight into possible methods of influencing news crews and politicians and our friends in denial to look as well.

Even if what we see doesn't push us to immediate action, it gives us information we'll need later. For instance, because I *have* seen *Schindler's List* six times, I can clearly recognize the parallels with the path the U.S. is taking now. And that does move me to action.

Maybe we'll never be brave enough to volunteer as security at a protest. Maybe we'll never even be "brave" enough to chant a slogan.

If we hope to accomplish anything positive at all, though, and let ourselves be moved to a deeper level of action, we have to be brave enough to watch a movie. Or, at the very least, a commercial during a break in *The Good Place*.

If Climate Change Is Real but Not Caused by Human Activity, Don't We Still Need to Address It?

(published in the *Salt Lake Tribune* on 23 June 2019)

Of all the baffling comments climate change deniers make, the one that astounds me most is their admission that yes, climate change "appears" to be real, but it isn't caused by human activity.

Even if humans aren't responsible for causing climate change, though, we're still going to do something about it, right? If scientists discovered that an asteroid was heading for Earth and would cause global destruction, are you saying that as long as it hadn't been sent on that collision course by humans, you wouldn't want to deflect it?

Many devout Christians believe that the Second Coming is imminent, and Jesus will fix everything when he arrives. To address climate change on our own would imply that we don't trust God to take care of us.

But God could conceivably perform some miracle right now to bring people to him. So are Mormon missionaries preaching in Italy, and Baptists preaching in Guatemala, and

Catholics preaching in Kenya implying that God can't take care of saving souls himself?

Despite the Amish opposition to electricity, and the opposition of Jehovah's Witnesses to blood transfusions, and that of Christian Scientists to medicine in general, most Christians have no problem accepting medical treatment or taking advantage of combustible engines or computers or any other scientific or technological advance.

So why do we draw the line at using science to solve a crisis that is already creating devastating floods and fires and famines at an ever-increasing pace? Especially when we know that our refusal to act will only make our lives exponentially more miserable later?

Part of it is the sunk cost fallacy. We've put a great deal into the status quo, and changing things will be so difficult and costly that it's easier to pretend the responsibility is someone else's, not ours.

But time and effort and money aren't the real issues, at least not for most voters fighting climate action. For them, the overriding reason they won't support Green New Deal candidates is that to do so would cause them to lose face.

This refusal to address a global climate crisis is the natural result of people trying to protect their fragile egos. But I'm not saying that disparagingly. This is a normal human reaction. The phrase "cutting off your nose to spite your face" didn't come out of nowhere.

When I tested positive for HIV, I dreaded the day I had to tell my family because I knew what it would mean. They'd express sympathy, but they'd do it with a gleam in their eye, feeling vindicated that God had punished me for leaving the Mormon Church. Painful as it was, I did tell them. Perhaps they didn't need to know, but I needed to live an honest life.

Opponents of fracking bans as well as bans on all new drilling and pipelines can convince themselves they are saving face through their opposition, but the thing is, the people they want to deceive can already see through them.

Four decades ago, one of my fellow missionaries wrote home weekly about all his incredible callings out in "the field." He told his friends and family he was a district leader, then a zone leader, then an assistant to the mission president. He did this even knowing that upon his arrival home, the bishop of his congregation would read a letter from the mission president specifying each position he'd actually held. My missionary colleague knew a day of reckoning was coming, but he kept lying anyway, because the benefits of lying were immediate while the consequences of being found out would only occur later.

Climate change is real. Whether or not it is caused by human activity, it is an existential crisis we must address. Climate change activists must not rub their "rightness" in the face of those we're trying to enlist. And climate change deniers need to accept their lumps and do the right thing.

Humiliation isn't fatal. But if we don't act now, there may be no plastic surgeons left the day we're ready to have them build the new noses we'll need.

Why We Hate Immigrants and What
We Can Do About It

Breaking up families. Putting children in pens. Letting desperate mothers die in the desert.

How can good, decent Americans commit such atrocities?

People do these things when they feel scared and violated.

Labeling our friends and neighbors evil does nothing to solve the humanitarian crisis at the border. Our conservative relatives aren't monsters. They are people who know they have it good and don't want additional people crowding in and ruining everything for everyone.

There's a little park in Seattle where I like to sit and meditate. It's beautiful and serene, a lovely sanctuary in the middle of a fast-paced city. But within three days of discovering this idyllic spot, I began to see chronically ill people wobbling in. They came with their canes and their walkers and their wheelchairs. It turned out the park was two blocks from a long-term care facility.

Clearly, the chronically ill park visitors were there before me, but I *felt* as if my beautiful sanctuary was being overrun. Not only were these "strangers" invading "my space," but they also had the audacity to talk and talk and talk.

Why couldn't they just go away?

Being chronically ill, some of them did, but I could hardly be happy about that.

My irrational territoriality is pretty much what most of us feel when the "invasion" is on a grander scale. I don't want four million visitors a year in Yellowstone. I don't want to cut down more forests for more houses for more people, even if those people are born to parents whose families have been U.S. citizens for 200 years.

I want *all* people to stop coming to the U.S. In fact, I want all people to stop coming to the entire planet. We're full up as it is.

And that's really the crux of the problem. Not only are there too many people on the planet, but the ones with more money and power exploit the rest, polluting and deforesting their land, installing dictators who oppress their own citizens while further enriching the wealthy.

Immigration isn't a problem only in the U.S. Most of Europe is reeling from the constant influx as well. As is Australia.

We've created many of the conditions that force millions of people from their homes. And then we're angered when they try to escape the misery we've helped create.

No one wants to think they're part of the problem. When I was a Mormon missionary, I didn't understand I was practicing cultural imperialism. I thought I was helping people. Now I see all the harm Mormon doctrine causes and wish I'd never been part of spreading it around the world.

We all *believed* coal and oil and gas were great things. Fossil fuels allowed us to achieve the miraculous.

But now we see the problems they cause. And one of those problems is mass immigration which will only worsen as the devastating effects of the climate crisis spread farther and wider across the planet.

We don't like hordes of immigrants coming to the U.S. and Canada and England and France and Italy and Germany? Then we better address the main culprit—fossil fuels.

I suppose another approach would be to kill everyone at the border. No money wasted on tents or food or medical care. No one "competing" for our jobs and clogging up our cities.

But is that really the kind of people we want to become? As much as I love my little park, I don't want to shove sick women in their wheelchairs in front of a bus.

Bottom line? If the reason we don't like unchecked immigration is because we're racist, if the reason is we just want to keep this beautiful space for ourselves, if the reason is we want to reserve it for our children only, if we have a unique reason all our own, it all comes down to this: we can only reduce immigration if we deal with the climate crisis.

If we don't, "they" will keep coming and coming and coming.

Are you a humanitarian? Then demand a shift to renewables.

Are you a selfish jerk? Then you need to demand a shift to renewables, too.

Whatever our personalities, whatever our political ideologies, we must all face the climate crisis head on if we expect to live in the country—or world—we want.

To Be an Ally or Not to Be

White activists should confront the epidemic of police killings of unarmed blacks. Straight folks should fight for LGBTQ rights. Christians should protest discrimination against Muslims. Men should demand passage of the Equal Rights Amendment.

Some oppressed or marginalized groups actively seek allies, but others see them as infiltrators complicit in their oppression. Rebuffing allies, though, is playing into the hands of those who keep their power by manipulating women and gays and blacks and Latinos and Native Americans to attack each other. Divide and conquer has been a successful strategy for centuries. We must resist the temptation to turn away allies and instead work to develop solidarity.

Shortly after I came out, I attended a Single Adult activity at church. One of the young women made a comment about a gay character on TV, a remarkable event back in the mid-1980s. "Can you believe how perverted the world is getting?" she asked.

I watched how my best friend, the only person in the room who knew my secret, reacted. He said nothing. Afterward, I asked him why.

He immediately grew angry. "People always want me to stick up for them! This is your fight, not mine!"

I suppose he was right, but I remember thinking, "How does an oppressed group ever gain any power if no one in the majority ever joins their fight?" Even as a closeted, self-loathing, celibate gay man, terrified of being found out, I stood up for gays. I could have done it during the Single Adult activity, but I wanted to see what my friend would do.

Or wouldn't do.

Some of my older white friends were Freedom Riders in the Deep South. They put their lives on the line. They don't want credit for it. They're happy to take a back seat. They would just prefer to be allowed to contribute to the cause of justice and equality without being vilified as "trying to make this about them."

I taught at a predominantly black university for ten years. A news report one day reported how a mob from a township in South Africa killed a white college student from California. "She was there to register blacks to vote," I said.

One of my students showed her disgust with my comment. "White people always think we need their help. They were right to kill her."

I understand rage. Being excommunicated from the Mormon Church for insisting on my right to seek love and companionship of my choosing left me bitter for years. Growing up in the south, where even "nice" people used the N-word, I was surprised the Rodney King riots in Los Angeles didn't spread across the entire country. Even with abundant exposure to black points of view, with years of interaction with blacks at all levels of society, I constantly discovered more layers of implicit bias I never realized I had.

Blacks certainly need to call us out when we do or say stupid or harmful things. To be clear, of course, it's not anyone else's job to teach us everything. There are tons of material we can access to teach ourselves. But we can't master all the information overnight, and we can't delay joining the fight for equality until we've perfected our knowledge and character.

Recently, a friend on Facebook posted a link to a new song by Taylor Swift called "You Need to Calm Down," where she stands up for gay rights. Some responded with an article from *The Onion.* "Taylor Swift Inspires Teen To Come Out As Straight Woman Needing To Be At Center Of Gay Rights Narrative." Then someone complained about Taylor Swift's father who was such "a monster" that the Indigo Girls wrote a song about him.

I don't think Taylor Swift is responsible for her father's behavior. I also don't think that because Taylor is a white, rich heterosexual that we should label her work as an ally self-serving. If her song serves us, I'm fine with it serving her as well.

I don't need perfect allies.

There are no perfect allies.

I'm not sure how effective Taylor Swift or anyone else would be if they had to take a vow of poverty or undergo conversion therapy before joining the fight.

We can correct or chastise or guide or debate, but it is self-defeating to toss allies into a moral waste bin.

In fourth grade, I saw a friend of mine being picked on during recess. A complete wimp then as now, I summoned up what little courage I had and walked up to the bullies. "Leave him alone," I said, using all the wit and wisdom at my disposal.

The bullies walked away, and my friend turned to me in anger. "I don't need your help!" he shouted before storming off.

I expect my friend was more embarrassed than angry, but even if I may have felt slightly hurt, my overwhelming reaction at the time was bewilderment. In his situation, I'd have welcomed any help I could get. And I'd been in his situation many times.

I saw *To Kill a Mockingbird* for the first time as an adult and immediately loved it. Many years would pass before I'd recognize the "white savior" issue. But I do wonder how else that story could have been told. Should a black lawyer have come to town? Should the black townspeople have rioted and burned the courthouse down? All viable options, I suppose. Stories can be told in many ways, and clearly more stories must be told from multiple black perspectives.

But white people have a stake in equality, too, and the character of Atticus Finch had every right to make what little contribution he could.

And really, the story isn't even about racism. That's just a vehicle for the real point, standing up to do the right thing even when most of your friends and peers are against you, even when you do it at great personal and professional risk. The point could have been made using homophobia instead of racism as the background. It could have been women's rights or anti-Semitism or pollution or anything else. It was the standing up that mattered, though using a black character as a vehicle for the white character to defy unjust societal norms is problematic as well. There's also the problem with Atticus dismissing the woman who claims to have been raped. I'm not sure Harper Lee used the best scenarios to make her point.

But I'm also not sure books and movies and authors have to be perfect to be useful.

The English movie *Pride* tells the true story of gay activists in the 1980's who rallied behind striking coal miners. Some gays refused to help, saying that the strikers were exactly the kind of guys who'd beaten them up as kids. Then lesbians broke from the group because they didn't want to be lumped with the men. And many of the strikers didn't want to be associated with either faggots *or* dykes.

After a homophobic union leader forces the gay activists out, other union supporters discover that the gay group has raised more money to support them than any other group.

Thirty years later, coal miners were among the strongest supporters when gay rights finally came up for a vote in the country.

"Androcles and the Lion" is effective as a fable because it tells a universal truth.

History has proven time and again that solidarity makes us stronger than we can ever be when we allow oppressors to divide us and waste our time and energy fighting each other instead of directing our energies against them.

No one wants to be undermined by an ally's misguided approach. Gay people don't want heterosexuals calling all the shots in their organizations. Women don't need men telling them the "right" way to protest. Blacks don't need whites ordering them about.

But debates over strategy and policy are essential. Allies need to be able to participate in those discussions, even if they aren't—and shouldn't be—in charge. Solidarity is always a work in progress, but the rewards are worth the effort.

I am a white gay male, an ex-Mormon atheist. Women's equality is essential for me if I'm to have a good life. Racial equality is essential for me to have a good life. Workers' rights are essential for me to have a good life.

When I lived in an economically depressed mobile home park with my first partner, one of the neighbors stopped by to tell us how he and some other neighbors had gotten together to confront yet another neighbor. "We told him to get rid of the black guy living with him or we'd burn him out." Our friendly neighbor laughed. "Isn't that great?"

I thought, "Yeah, the two gay guys are thrilled to hear about violent bigotry."

Martin Luther King, Jr. stated it clearly. "Injustice anywhere is a threat to justice everywhere."

I have a moral obligation to help oppressed groups to which I don't belong.

I also have self-interest.

Members of every oppressed group need to fight for their rights. Members of every other oppressed group, and every decent human being belonging to every privileged group, must join together in solidarity to fight for the rights of all who don't have them now. Equality and justice aren't scarce resources.

The more we give to more people, the more there is for everyone.

We can't abdicate our responsibility out of fear we'll be reprimanded and embarrassed. Let's be the best allies we can be, and let's accept the imperfect help offered to us in our own battles anywhere we can find it.

Taxpayer Dollars Should Benefit All Citizens

Whenever some controversial humanitarian subject comes up, we can expect to hear right-wing conservatives complaining about the use of their taxes. "I don't want my tax dollars funding abortion!" "I don't want my tax dollars paying gay teachers!" "I don't want my tax dollars supporting welfare for people too lazy to work!"

I wasn't aware we got to pick and choose where our individual tax dollars went. And I wasn't aware that right-wing taxpayers were funding all these programs single-handedly.

Why do conservatives get to defund Planned Parenthood, yet I have to use my money to support murdering civilians in Afghanistan? Why do conservatives get to defund research on climate change and gun deaths and stem cells, yet I have to pay subsidies to fossil fuel companies? Why do conservatives get to prevent their taxes from supporting public schools in poor areas, yet I have to use my taxes to support Trump's hotels?

We aren't talking about one or two instances of inequity in the way our taxes our spent. Consistently, right-wing conservatives get to direct *our* money, both on the state and federal level, but we can't direct theirs (or ours).

Why, for instance, do conservatives get to refuse funding for universal healthcare, yet we have to fund the world's most bloated military budget? Conservatives get to defund PBS, but we have to pay for the death penalty. Conservatives get to refuse funding for childcare, but we have to pay to support the largest prison system per capita in the world. Conservatives get to deny funding for tuition-free colleges and trade schools, but we have to pay to build sports stadiums and bail out banks. They can abandon Puerto Rico and the homeless, but we must subsidize pharmaceutical companies that artificially raise the price of life-saving medication by 400%, 600%, even 1000%.

Churches and other religious institutions don't have to pay any taxes at all but are allowed to lobby for laws and policies that affect how the tax money the rest of us pay is spent.

When I used to fill out a donation slip in my Mormon congregation, I could mark where I wanted my funds to go. To the poor in my congregation, to the maintenance of our building, to a fund supporting volunteer missionaries, to build a temple a few hours closer to my state, or to Church headquarters to be distributed as they thought best. If conservatives want the IRS to add three or four pages at the end of our returns listing some of the programs or departments where we can direct 50% or 60% of our income tax, let's debate and make sure *everyone* gets the same options. Maybe that would work, and maybe it wouldn't, but defunding or minimally funding almost every humanitarian program in the country certainly isn't making America great again.

Yeah, I get that conservatives don't want their money supporting every single item in the budget. *No one does.* But living in a society that has to serve *all* its citizens means having to put up with some of our money going to projects or policies we don't like. We should certainly debate the best use of limited funds, but the assumption that one party gets to unilaterally decide that *only* their needs are met and no one else's is far from the American ideal conservatives claim to uphold.

Conservatives, take a breath and relax. You *are* getting to spend your tax dollars the way you want *far* more than those of us on the left. Chill out, already. You're winning. Are you really so needy—and petty—that you can't let us at least have a few crumbs? Even Antoinette offered the peasants cake.

Not enough, of course, but then, we all know how that turned out.

If conservatives want a society where they can be happy, they are going to have to contribute to a society where the rest of us have a fighting chance as well.

E pluribus unum, guys. We're all in this together.

Mormons Hate Socialism, But Only in the United States

(published in the *Salt Lake Tribune* on 12 August 2018 and included in *Human Compassion for Beginners*)

Almost every day, one of my active Mormon family members posts some scathing comment on Facebook about the evils of Socialism. One day, it's a clip of Meghan McCain dissing Democratic Socialism. Another day, he makes fun of liberal idiots who don't know the difference between Democratic Socialism and real Socialism. The day after that, he posts a meme saying, "Socialism can be summed up in a single sentence: Hate the man that is better off than you are."

I find his venom odd given that early in LDS Church history, the saints attempted to live the United Order. And during the temple endowment, Mormons agree to live the United Order again if ever required.

The Book of Mormon makes clear that the Nephites lived some form of Socialism after Christ visited them, for a good two hundred years. And that this was the only time in the entire book where the people lived in complete peace and happiness.

U.S. Mormons I know say that it's okay if the Church wants to implement some form of Socialism, but governments are secular and will contaminate anything good they try to do.

That begs the question of why secular Capitalist governments are to be praised specifically for their Capitalism.

I don't recall passages from the Book of Mormon lauding Capitalist practices. If anything, the scriptures suggest that it was the return to non-Socialist practices that brought about the destruction of the Nephites.

The main reason Mormons in the United States rail against anything Socialist is because so much of their "doctrine" is derived from the Republican Party.

Republicans hate any form of universal healthcare not because it's ineffective but because it's Socialist. Yet Mormons in England, and France, and Japan, and in all the other countries with such programs don't have to denounce their country's healthcare system and insist on for-profit healthcare in order to obtain temple recommends, do they?

Do Mormons in countries with tuition-free college have to travel to the U.S. for their education rather than accept the Socialist-provided instruction at home? If they don't, will they still be worthy to serve missions?

My Mormon family member also posts memes which clearly reflect the Republican influence on his moral values. One reads, "Can you still own a firearm with a straw conviction in California?" thus combining his disdain for environmental conservation with his refusal to approve even one solitary gun regulation that might decrease the massacres which take place routinely in the U.S.

Do Mormons who live in countries that promote renewable energy have to defy their country's emissions standards if they want to attend their child's temple wedding? Must Mormons in countries with strict gun regulations buy guns on the black market to be set apart as bishop or Relief Society president?

In between his posts vilifying the left, my family member intersperses quotes from various Church leaders. One from Bonnie Oscarson reads, "We must stop concentrating on our differences and look for what we have in common."

Then come two posts ranting about how awful Black athletes are who protest police officers killing unarmed Blacks during routine traffic stops.

Republican Mormons in the United States seem to feel they have to support every cruel, inhumane, and destructive "moral imperative" that the Republican Party endorses, even when those policies are in defiance of Church history and scripture, even though Mormons in other parts of the world have little or no problem with Socialist or Democratic Socialist or plain old mainstream ideas. Yet most Mormons in the U.S. would flatly deny their views are shaped by politics.

I remember being surprised on my mission to discover that one of our most faithful missionaries, a young Italian woman, was a committed Communist. She also remained a committed Mormon until her death 35 years later.

I think many Mormons are misquoting the statement at the beginning of this essay. The original must read, "Capitalism can be summed up in a single sentence: Hate the man that is worse off than you are." It is the poor, the uneducated, the immigrant, the sick who must be denied a society that would make them equal in any way to "good" people like themselves.

Or: "Don't love thy neighbor as thyself."

People lament every day about those who put party over country. I'm looking forward to the time Mormons stop putting party over morality.

We Forgot What "Never Forget" Means

"Godwin's Law" tells us that the longer an online discussion continues, the more likely someone will make a comparison to Nazis or to Hitler. This "law" is brought up instantly to ridicule anyone who invokes such comparisons, even when those comparisons are apt. Rather than be shamed from using the memory of one of the most horrible periods of the twentieth century as a tool to prevent the repeat of such atrocities, we need to feel empowered to use those comparisons every time they're appropriate. If we allow others to censor us, we've forgotten what "Never Forget" means.

When I converted to Judaism in the mid-1990s, I learned that a member of the synagogue I was affiliated with was an Auschwitz survivor. I was too intimidated to talk with her. She was a mythic figure. It was like meeting Elizabeth Bennet or Sherlock Holmes or some other famous fictional character. I'd read dozens of books on the Holocaust and knew, of course, that it was real, but meeting a death camp survivor in person made it real in a way it hadn't been before.

Many of us are so far removed from World War II that reading about it or even watching movies is like picking up *The Iliad* or *The Odyssey*.

When I was 11, I saw horrifying pictures on the front page of my local newspaper, *The Times-Picayune*. A charred leg sticking out of a window with a burned corpse in the background. A burned man's head and arms protruding from another window where he died trying to escape an arson in a French Quarter gay bar.

But the most haunting image was that of a survivor down on the sidewalk looking up in horror as his friends burned to death.

In 1991, the Louisiana State Museum opened an exhibit in the Presbytère on Jackson Square detailing the worst fires in New Orleans history.

The Upstairs Lounge fire was not mentioned, despite killing 32 people, far more than any other fire profiled in the exhibit. Even two devastating fires which destroyed large parts of the city early in its history caused fewer deaths.

When LGBTQ folk aren't important enough to remember, their lives and rights aren't important enough to protect.

A reporter once asked me what impact those photos had on the gay community in New Orleans over the next two or three decades.

"They had no impact," I said. "The gay community didn't know they existed." In the days before the internet, photos such as those disappeared from the world after the newspapers went out in the trash. A few people might see preserved copies, but by the time I did my research on the fire fifteen years later, only survivors or friends and relatives of those killed remembered the tragedy had even happened.

Despite all the Holocaust literature I had consumed over the years, it wasn't until I read *The Men with the Pink Triangle* that I realized gays, Roma, Jehovah's Witnesses, and other "criminals" were sent to the camps as well. It wasn't until after I came out that I discovered gay men liberated from the camps at the end of the war were then transferred to regular prisons.

Never forget? How can we forget something we never knew?

As a former Mormon, I know Mormons love to celebrate their history, particularly when it involves heroism or martyrdom. And yet it wasn't until I was no longer even Jewish that I learned of German teenager Helmuth Hübener, a Mormon who was arrested for working against the Nazis.

Before Hübener's execution, he was excommunicated by the leader of his Mormon congregation, the man who'd made no effort to protect another congregant, a Jew who'd converted to Mormonism, allowing without protest the former Jew to be carted off to his death. David Conley Nelson's *Moroni and the Swastika* reveals a significant number of German Mormons who supported the Nazi regime.

This is especially important for Mormons to remember, given the large percentage that support President Trump and his awful policies.

Jews are protesting concentration camps along our southern border.

Even Mike Godwin says that there are times when breaking his "law" is necessary. After a white supremacist mowed down a protester in Charlottesville, he said, "By all means, compare these shitheads to Nazis."

Denying protesters and activists the right to use the lessons of history to prevent atrocities in our time isn't "protecting" the memory of those killed in the Holocaust. It's a call of a different kind, a call every bit as dangerous as forgetting. "Never give a damn!"

Did Dinosaurs Dance?

Gay people can be homophobic. Women can be misogynists. Blacks can experience internalized racial inferiority. But I don't think I'm being ageist when I say we don't need dinosaurs leading the Democratic Party.

Dianne Feinstein, Nancy Pelosi, and Joe Biden are just a few of the older political "leaders" who are holding back younger folks like Alexandria Ocasio-Cortez and Rashida Tlaib. They're also trying to suppress older people like Bernie Sanders and Elizabeth Warren who have fresh, energetic ideas.

Just as older folks have the option of either embracing technology or becoming Luddites, politicians and voters of all ages have a choice between remaining centrist moderates or taking on the future.

There was a time society could function even with oppressive economic and environmental policies. There was a time civilization could prosper with slavery and the disenfranchisement of women and people of color.

There was a time when Blockbuster Video could flourish, when the film industry could ignore black American viewers or Chinese citizens, when Union Carbide could kill thousands in Bhopal, India without most Americans blinking an eye.

As much as some people might like to go back to that enchanted *Leave It to Beaver* era when blacks were lynched almost weekly, that's no longer a world that can function. The increase of billions of people since that time and the rapidly escalating climate crisis have changed both the physical and political landscape.

I read Sir Arthur Conan Doyle's *The Lost World* as a child. I read *The Enormous Egg*. When I learned basic needle arts as a child, I drew designs of dinosaurs on pillow cushions and embroidered them. As an adult, I read both Michael Crichton novels about *Jurassic Park*, and I loved both the first and third movies in the franchise. I took a Dinosaur course in college.

While a fan of the original *Star Trek* and *Star Trek: The Next Generation*, I found that one of my favorite episodes of any of the various Star Trek series was Season 3: Episode 23 of *Star Trek: Voyager*, where we discover that one species of hadrosaur managed to emigrate sometime in Earth's distant past and colonize another planet.

Most of us love dinosaurs. Somehow, in some unexplainable way, we identify with them.

I also identify with gay Mormons who buy into the homophobia they are taught by their Church. But I made the decision a long time ago not to choose a life of sexual self-loathing. I don't need to identify to the point of self-destruction.

I don't own a cell phone. I don't download music. I don't read ebooks. I make old man noises when I get up, if I can get up at all.

Browsing YouTube, which I only recently discovered, I found a video of a cockatoo that has 14 different dance moves as it listens to Cyndi Lauper's "Girls Just Wanna Have Fun." A quick search revealed another two dozen videos of birds breaking into spontaneous dance moves to music. And we all know about birds that perform elaborate, choreographed mating dances.

Since birds evolved from the one surviving branch of dinosaurs, one has to wonder if any dinosaurs, avian or non-avian, ever danced. When T-rex bust a gut, was it with his tapping feet rather than his teeth? Did velociraptors have dance troupes?

I like Dianne Feinstein. I like Nancy and Joe.

And I absolutely love my wooden dinosaur carvings from Bali, though I gaze at them with a feeling of melancholy and regret, understanding that cutting down the trees to carve them only exacerbated the deterioration of our climate.

If Democrats are going to survive as a political party, if America is going to survive as a democracy (or even a republic), if the West is going to survive technological tyranny and political oligarchy, if civilization itself is going to survive the climate crisis, we can't keep thinking like Oviraptors.

When I watch the video of Alexandria Ocasio-Cortez dancing on the roof, I see a survivor, part of the branch of humans embracing rather than fighting evolution.

Dinosaurs like Pelosi and Feinstein and Biden need to move to the left or get out of the way.

But if they don't, I hope at least some birds survive our current mass extinction event. The Spix's macaw, made famous by the movie *Rio*, didn't, but I hope cockatoos will.

The Desensitized Sensibilities of Pro-Life Activists

Pro-life activists post sweet photographs of babies to show everyone what is lost when a woman or girl undergoes an abortion. They talk of fetal pain, of fetal heartbeats, of the sanctity of life. But they will be more effective at persuading those who support a woman's right to make decisions about her own womb if they use their *real* arguments, the ones that convinced *them*.

If it's cruel to inflict pain on one's child (or any child), how can a parent vaccinate their child against measles? How can they subject their three-year-old with leukemia to chemotherapy or bone marrow transplants? How can these folks, who are often in favor of corporal punishment, even spank a disobedient toddler?

If the degree of innocence of those suffering the pain is the issue, I hear that women and girls who are pregnant as a result of rape often feel pain during childbirth. They can feel it during conception and pregnancy as well. If the "innocent" life of a fetus trumps the "sinful" pain of a pregnant woman, I have to wonder if a woman impregnated by her husband is really the slut this attitude suggests.

If we're trying to prevent pain in general, innocent or not, I wonder why so many of the folks against abortion are also those who support torture, an international war crime.

Even pro-life activists who aren't so extreme still largely seem to be the folks adamantly against food programs for the poor, which of course includes millions of children not the least bit responsible for the poverty they're experiencing. Do they understand that chronic hunger is painful? If it's a sin to abort a fetus with severe physical or mental abnormalities, why is it morally acceptable to force the birth of that child, knowing many of these abnormalities will ensure the child a lifetime of pain?

One wonders if pro-life activists consider the validity of emotional pain. Like that of knowing you're bringing a life into the world you can't afford to feed. Wagging a finger at these women and shouting, "You should have thought of that before you spread your legs!" doesn't alleviate her pain or the suffering of that child. It doesn't seem to function well as a deterrent, either.

What about the emotional pain of being forced to carry and deliver the child of your rapist? Or the unwanted child of the husband you love? Even women who aren't raped, women who have never had sex with anyone other than their husbands, still often have little or no access to contraception, especially when their employers are allowed to deny insurance coverage that might pay for it, or if the women are morally appropriate stay-at-home moms who don't have an employer to provide coverage in the first place. And if you're poor, reliant on public transportation, and you don't have the financial resources to feed the kids you already have, it's hard to find the time or money or energy to drag your kids to the drugstore so you can buy spermicidal jelly.

In fairy tales, the stories often end with marriage and a promise that the couple will live "happily ever after." Anyone who's actually been married, though, understands that the wedding ceremony is the beginning of a long, arduous journey, not the end of one. Pro-life activists care a great deal about ensuring the birth of a child, but then they wash their hands of responsibility. They don't support guaranteed childcare, guaranteed healthcare, or anything else that might support that new life. "Those things aren't the government's responsibility!" they insist. Odd, isn't it, how feeding, housing, and providing medical care for children is government interference, but forcing women and girls to bear these children isn't.

Clearly, banning abortion in an effort to legislate away pain cannot possibly be the real motivation.

The only reason to ban abortion, it seems, is because pro-life activists really are pro-life. They work hard to ensure that every unwanted child is delivered into the hands of an uncaring world because they recognize the sanctity of life above all else, including love, health, comfort, and happiness.

Yet while the survival of a fetus with a heartbeat is mandatory, making sure that the heart of an already-born human *keeps* beating is nowhere on the list of moral imperatives. Do you need medication for a heart condition? Too bad. So sad. You had a chance at a heartbeat when you were still in a legally mandated womb. You can't expect us to do *everything* for you.

Some pro-life activists insist that "dignity" is their motivation. The fetus deserves the dignity to make up its own mind whether or not it wants to live. Obviously, a fetus can't make that decision, so we have to ensure it survives to the age of eighteen when as an adult he or she will have the right to commit suicide.

This pretense is even more preposterous and seems only a minimally disguised version of the "heartbeat" argument. What pro-life activist out there is advocating for aid in dying for physically healthy young adults wanting to commit suicide? They're not rallying for universal counseling or psychiatric care, either.

The Bill of Rights promises us the right to life, liberty, and the pursuit of happiness. But most pro-life activists only seem to want to guarantee the right to a low quality of life.

It's curious that so many of these activists are also those in support of the death penalty. Against giving their children HPV vaccinations. Of sending others off to war. Eager themselves to kill in war. And so silent when Jews, Muslims, blacks, or LGBT folk are killed by police or terrorists or plain old regular murderers.

It's almost as if they believe only *some* lives have sanctity. That only *some* people should have the liberty to pursue happiness.

Eliminating pain isn't the real goal. Ensuring that heartbeats continue isn't the real goal. Caring about life itself isn't the real goal. Pro-life activists need to understand that pro-choice supporters can *see* that those aren't the real goals. If pro-life activists want to convince their opponents, they'll need to tell the truth.

So what *is* the real goal?

Well, let's be honest. There are two basic reasons, and neither of them is politically correct.

But screw political correctness! Pro-life activists represent God, and they don't need to be ashamed of telling it like it is!

The first reason to ban abortion is to punish women and girls for having sex. Even those who were raped somehow provoked the rapists into assaulting them. Pro-life activists understand the sexual appeal of 10-year-old girls like no one else. Rapists may be bad, but ultimately, women and girls are responsible for their rape and, by extension, their pregnancy.

By God, they have to *pay* for that.

Plus, if we can turn desperate pregnant women and their doctors into felons over abortion, there's the added bonus that these "liberals" will be disenfranchised in most states from voting. What better way to guarantee we get the right elected officials in office to legislate on the rest of the conservative agenda?

And what's the second main reason to ban abortion?

It's the fact that when all is said and done, a woman's true function in life is to be a wife and mother. It's perhaps minimally acceptable if a woman wants to be a teacher or a nurse or maid, but we can only tolerate such nonsense if the woman knows her real place. A pregnant host devoting her life to childrearing, completely dependent on a man, is God's universal path for women.

The fundamental, overriding impulse pushing pro-life activists to ban every abortion possible is their desire to support God's command to keep women subject to men.

If pro-life activists want to persuade pro-choice supporters, they are going to have to be honest about it.

But, you know, those of us who support a woman's right to choose *already* understand the real motivation.

So what's a pro-life activist to do?

Perhaps the best option is to let compassion guide your life rather than the compulsion to force universal adherence to your personal religious beliefs. You can still be a faithful believer without implementing an Inquisition that puts women and doctors in prison, that enslaves women to decades of servitude to children *you'll* never have to lift another finger to help.

I attended a Baptist high school for four years, where all students, Baptist or not, were required to attend "chapel," take a year-long Bible course taught by the pastor's wife, and attend Sunday services in exchange for an extra three days of Thanksgiving break. I was a Mormon missionary for two years, during which my personal worth was measured by how many lessons I taught, how many "investigators" I brought to church, and how many families I dunked in the baptismal font. I *get* wanting everyone to live the gospel as you see it. If you want to preach to me, pray for me, set an example for me, by all means go for it. Just be honest about what you really want and why.

You are not concerned about children. I'm afraid the evidence is incontrovertible. What you want is to play God. If you can explain why we should accept your coup taking over

God's rule, perhaps you can win us all over to your side voluntarily.

But wouldn't it be better if you just repented and re-sensitized your own desensitized sensibilities instead?

Our Climate Loan Has Come Due

We took out an environmental loan by using fossil fuels even after understanding the havoc they were causing. We've fallen behind on our payments, and now the lender is demanding we settle our debt in full.

When I started my Biology degree, I didn't have much money. I'd paid for my BA in English with money I inherited from my mother. I paid for my MA in English by teaching a few composition classes in exchange for tuition. I managed to pay for my MFA while I took classes as well. But I had to take out student loans to pursue my Biology degree. I was warned repeatedly to take out as little as possible because I'd have to pay it all back one day. "Be careful," I was told. "Be smart." "Think ahead." "There will be a day of reckoning."

But I took out the max allowed every semester. I was paying the rent and utilities and everything else by myself. I still needed a full income even while attending school. I *couldn't* "be smart." I *couldn't* think of the future. I was trying to get through this month's bills. I hoped to get a good job upon graduation. Or maybe I'd win the lottery. Somehow, I'd find a way to deal with the debt later.

I owed $48,000 by the time I graduated. That was nineteen years ago. I didn't get a good job. I didn't win the lottery. I still owe almost $18,000 despite making payments every month. It was only about a year ago that I was five days late for the first time, and the lender raised my interest rate as a penalty. Permanently.

We've long known that using fossil fuels was going to cause devastation down the line. But we needed electricity to run our refrigerators. We needed gasoline to get to work. We knew we'd regret it one day, but we were so overwhelmed by our immediate needs that we couldn't let ourselves worry about the future.

I can include my mortgage payment in bankruptcy proceedings if I need to. I can include my car loan. I can include my credit card.

But I can't include my student loan. I *have* to pay that whether I want to or not. And if I refuse, the lender can garnish my wages. There is no escaping that debt.

Progressive policy changes on tuition and student loan debt might eventually help students, but even the most progressive policy changes on fossil fuels cannot erase the debt we owe to the planet.

Student loans are crippling. I knew they would be and took them out anyway. So perhaps we can forgive ourselves for being foolish about our use of fossil fuels. But like it or not, our environmental loan has come due and we must repay it. The interest rate is already high, but the lender can—and will—raise it even higher if we don't pay immediately.

The human mind is capable of creating lovely sonnets. It's capable of studying epibatidine. We're smart and creative. But we're also good at denial. Like a man who knows his husband is cheating on him but who can pretend it isn't true as long as the words aren't said out loud, we can know and not know something essential at the same time. We've long understood there would be a day of reckoning for our use of fossil fuels. We said we'd deal with it then.

That then is now.

Give Me Your Tired, Your Poor, Your Europeans

(published in *LA Progressive* on 15 August 2019)

Ken Cuccinelli recently said out loud what most supporters of a wall along the U.S. southern border have already shown they believe. The US Citizenship and Immigration Services Director told reporters that the famous poem by Emma Lazarus on the base of the Statue of Liberty only applied to Europeans. They are therefore, he implied, the only acceptable immigrants to our country. But that really begs an obvious question—aren't Mexicans and other Latin American immigrants largely of European descent?

Latin American peoples clearly descend from three main groups. Most countries south of the U.S. border are Spanish-speaking because of the heavy Spanish influx in their past. Brazil, of course, had a large Portuguese influence. No one should have to point out that Spain and Portugal are European nations. So why aren't *those* European people acceptable?

The other large component of Latin American DNA is, of course, indigenous Native Americans.

It feels like a stretch to say that Americans are unacceptable immigrants to America. Mexico is, after all, part of North *America*. Immigrants from Guatemala and Honduras and El

Salvador are from Central America. Immigrants from Colombia and Venezuela and countries farther south are from South America.

All are, by definition, Americans. You'd think that would count for as much as being descended from Cossacks or Nazis or Vikings. Even Belgians, who we often associate with Hercule Poirot or the lovely city of Bruges, led a murderous regime that killed over ten million people.

Of course, the ten million killed were dark-skinned people in the Congo, so apparently Belgian immigrants get a pass.

Even if we consider The United States of America the only *real* America, surely we know that a huge portion of the present-day western and southwestern United States belonged to Mexico before it belonged to the U.S. The battle of the Alamo happened in Mexico, not the U.S. Mormons immigrated to Mexico to establish Salt Lake City, not to "Utah." Florida and parts of Alabama, Mississippi, and Louisiana belonged to Spain before they belonged to the U.S. The French Quarter of New Orleans was not always French.

Are we splitting hairs—or DNA strands—to insist that only the darker Europeans or their descendants don't qualify as "real" Europeans?

Most white Americans today aren't European, either. They're *descendants* of Europeans, just like many of the people entering the country across our southern border through our official ports of entry.

Cuccinelli didn't stop there with his rewriting of both poetry and history. He pointed out that "The New Colossus" wasn't affixed to the Statue of Liberty until *after* a law was established requiring that all new immigrants be able to "stand on their own two feet" with no public support before being allowed into the country.

Anti-immigrants fail to recognize the questions this assertion raises as well. If we require immigrants to support themselves, why are we so insistent they not be given jobs? And if we're more worried that they're freeloaders who don't want jobs in the first place, why are we raiding workplaces in order to round them up for deportation?

The faulty logic in these arguments points to the real forces behind anti-immigrant animosity—scapegoating and bigotry.

Unfortunately, logic doesn't engage the masses. Emotion does. And given the coldness with which many anti-immigrant voters react to the photos of children in cages, of ICE agents tearing fathers from their families, of immigrants drowning in their attempt to reach our country, of immigrants (and Mexican shoppers only in town briefly to pick up a few things at Walmart) being gunned down as they shield their children, it's going to be a task of monumental proportions to revive a functioning conscience in many of them.

Because even reading this, their hearts are not touched but seem to only grow colder.

Öl Macht Frei

(published in *LA Progressive* on 27 May 2019)

My father was a tractor pull champion. A homebuilder by trade, his office walls were lined with dozens of shiny trophies. He was Texas state champion in his category. When he retired from building, he moved back to his farm, converting one field to a staging area where he could host his own tractor pulls. This was fun for him. It was validating. He was able to socialize, make some money, and feel important.

What's wrong with any of that?

Not much, really, except that each tractor could burn through an entire tank of gas in minutes.

Fossil fuel corporations are our biggest adversary in transitioning to other forms of energy that release less carbon into the atmosphere, but the biggest obstacle in getting "the people" to take those corporations down is the impact on our personal lives. My nephew works for an oil company and has been able to provide a comfortable living for his family for the past 15 years. A smart guy, he never graduated from high school. The only job I remember him working before his current position was one painting cars. He also likes tractor pulls.

My nephew has several children he loves deeply. Each day he goes to work, he is condemning them to a harsher and harsher future. But he won't stop because to do so would put them in dire circumstances *today*.

Back when I was Mormon, my bishop worked for Shell Oil as a geologist. I'd long enjoyed geology, but he pointed out that it was difficult to earn money as a geologist unless you were searching for oil. That didn't particularly appeal to me, even in the days before I had heard about global warming. My bishop eventually became my stake president and presided over my Court of Love where I was excommunicated for being gay. As he pulled me into a separate room away from the group of high priests who'd convicted me, he said, "I know some great guys at work who are gay. I don't know why the Church has this position, but I don't have any choice but to excommunicate you."

Good people do terrible things because they feel they don't have options. We will be unable to persuade the public to go along with the disruptive changes required not only to cease carbon emissions but also to recapture tons of it already released. That means we must take a multi-issue approach.

Tuition-free colleges and trade schools would help workers shift to new careers. But my nephew would not be able to attend any educational program for two to four or six years without being able to provide for his family in the meantime. We need an adequate stipend for the time it takes folks to shift to other jobs. We need guaranteed childcare as well. And no one is going to leave a secure position if they have to worry about medical bills. We can't cut our dependence on fossil fuels unless we implement single-payer or some other form of universal healthcare.

Our survival depends on a sweeping overhaul of our entire culture and economy. It's daunting. Deep into the world's sixth mass extinction event, the only one caused by human activity, we've just seen another sobering report on global warming. An additional million species will soon be added to the already staggering death toll.

Many brave souls fought against the Nazi regime, but many more did not, afraid that fighting back would guarantee their deaths while waiting it out might give them a chance to survive. The sign above the entrance to Auschwitz promised that work would make them free. They clung to the promise, even as they marched to the gas chambers.

The entrances to all fossil fuel companies, their storage facilities, and the work sites that process or transport those fossil fuels should have new signs erected over them.

"Öl macht frei."

Unless we can offer those who make their living bringing death to the world a viable alternative, they will keep doing their jobs. Blaming them for their short-sightedness is both unfair and unhelpful. If we really want to save ourselves, we can't tackle this challenge one piece at a time. A sizable chunk of the funds necessary to implement these radical changes can be requisitioned from the massive fossil fuel subsidies and tax breaks we currently give to fossil fuel corporations. The rest can be redirected from our bloated military budget.

Since 1945, we've dreaded what World War III would look like. Well, it's here. The entire planet is facing an enemy greater than we've ever known. And it will take a massive, multi-faceted attack to achieve victory.

Nothing to Fear but Fearmongering Itself

Mexicans are murderers and rapists!

Muslims are terrorists!

Iran is going to nuke us!

Black thugs are out to rob and kill us!

Socialists want to destroy America!

A full list of Donald Trump's lies designed to rile up his base would take pages. Everyone wants a protector when they're afraid. And researchers have shown that the brains of conservatives react more strongly—and differently—to fear than those of others.

Leftists can be afraid, too, of course. We're afraid of what Trump and his hateful policies are doing to the people of our country. We're afraid he'll initiate a war the way George W. Bush scared people into believing Iraq had Weapons of Mass Destruction. We're afraid an escalated "War on Terror" will waste trillions more dollars we desperately need to address problems here at home. We're afraid of Trump's anti-science crusade escalating rather than curbing the climate crisis.

There's plenty of fear to go around.

The difference is that the fear those of us on the left experience doesn't lead us to oppress others. Instead, it pushes us to stop polluting the Earth. It encourages us to stand up for the unjustly imprisoned. When our brains register fear, we work to protect voting rights, to demand universal healthcare, to protect the right to protest, to insist that police stop killing unarmed blacks.

Fear can be useful if we channel it to do good.

But Trump manipulates his followers to do bad. It's not that the followers themselves are bad. Not all of them, anyway. The neo-Nazis? Yeah, they're bad. But I know many Trump supporters in my family to be good, decent people.

Until their fear drives them to support awful, terrible policies.

But labeling all Trump supporters evil is counterproductive at best. We can never persuade anyone while belittling them. It's possible that neither logic nor an appeal to their better emotions will work, either, but that's all we've got, unless we think the "final solution" to the problem of conservatives vs. liberals is civil war.

And let's face it, they've probably got more guns than we do.

So let's try de-escalation.

A police officer may be a good family man. He may go to church every Sunday. He may donate to medical research and work hard to make his community safe. But in that split second during a routine traffic stop when he feels threatened, his instinct for self-preservation kicks in, and he may do something awful, something irrevocable, something he regrets for the rest of his life. But he does it anyway, because he's acting out of fear.

We can't fire every fearful police officer who supports Trump. We can't indict every right-wing conservative acting out of fear. If we imprison too many people in this country already, what would a country locking up an additional 25,000,000 people look like?

Fear led people to hang "witches" in Salem. It led to the Rosewood massacre. It led to the internment of U.S. citizens of Japanese descent during World War II.

Unfounded but deeply felt fear led to widespread hysteria when Orson Welles broadcast a radio version of *War of the Worlds*, people terrified by a piece of fiction into believing they were about to be murdered by aliens.

When buffalo panic, they stampede, trampling and killing anyone in their path. Horses are dangerous when they stampede, too. And so are humans.

Fear, justified or not, has life and death consequences.

Let's start using strategies developed by Terror Management Theory to calm down the fearful Trump supporters in our lives. Let's take de-escalation courses offered by our employers or community centers. Let's stop writing nasty, derisive comments on posts our family and friends make.

Our nation is still divided today 150 years after the end of the Civil War, showing we can't "eliminate" everyone on the other side, even if we wanted to (and I hope to God we don't want to). If we are going to have to live with people motivated to do awful things out of fear, our only hope is to find ways to lessen that fear without provoking terror as we do it.

We want a quick fix, but there just may not be one. No law or policy or Supreme Court ruling can mandate that people stop experiencing unjustified fear. If we don't like watching hate in action, we have to be the ones to turn it around one person at a time with patience, kindness and, yes, ridiculous as it sounds, love.

My Mother's Forced Abortion and Sterilization

(published in *LA Progressive* on 13 July 2019)

When my sister was pregnant with her first child back in 1976, we teased her with the movie *It's Alive!* in which a mutant baby with claws and fangs kills the entire medical team that helps deliver it within moments of its birth.

My sister and I didn't realize at the time that *we* were the killer offspring. My best friends were killer offspring. My Sunday School teachers were killer offspring. My Mormon bishop, who worked for an oil company, was a major killer offspring.

For a nation that seems to be increasingly pro-life, we seem to have no problem aborting the offspring of virtually every other life form.

The majority of Americans are urban dwellers or, at their most rural, suburbanites. We visit parks or grow a few flowers in our front yard, maybe a vegetable or two in a window box, but for the most part, we've lost our connection to nature: continually pregnant with new life—spring buds, fruiting blackberry bushes, robins laying eggs, cows calving, corn ready to harvest for eating or for gathering seeds for the next generation.

But so many Americans who are adamantly pro-life when it comes to human fetuses are fine with aborting the life Mother Nature attempts to bring into the world. We clear cut old growth forests to establish palm oil plantations to flavor our chips. We block salmon breeding grounds with dams. We hunt whales to extinction. We blithely continue using pesticides we know kill bees. Once those bees are gone, hundreds of plant species that depend on them will join their fate within a single pollinating season. And when those plants go, so do the essential foods human rely on to fill our plates...and bellies.

When we hear about a teenage girl abandoning her newborn in a dumpster, we're ready to burn her at the stake. If the death of that baby qualifies as infanticide rather than abortion, the problem is that many pro-life activists conflate the two all the time. Pro-life lawmakers force women to hold burials for miscarried fetuses. Abortion is compared to the Holocaust. Over 60 million abortions have been performed in the U.S. since Roe vs. Wade. That makes pro-choice voters worse than Nazis.

The direct human death toll from the Exxon Valdez oil spill, the Deepwater Horizon spill, and dozens of others can't possibly compare to death camp totals. But do the lives of the 250,000 birds, the loss of billions of salmon and herring eggs, and the countless other animals killed when the Valdez left 1300 miles of coastline covered in oil count? Do the lives of the one million birds and hundreds of thousands of other animals killed by the BP oil spill count? Does the incalculable number of lives lost in the 1000+ other oil spills in the U.S. count? Those killed in oil spills around the rest of the globe?

An oil train derailed in Lac-Mégantic in the province of Quebec, Canada, burning half the downtown and leaving 47 people dead. All but three of the surviving downtown buildings had to be demolished because of petroleum contamination. Over 1200 people were killed by a series of pipeline explosions in Nigeria. I hope the thousands of coal miners killed in dozens and dozens of mine disasters count for something, too.

We're horrified by the ethical implications of using stem cells harvested from aborted fetuses to develop cures for diseases that affect the rest of us. We're conflicted when parents choose to bring another child into the world for the primary purpose of providing a bone marrow transplant for their already-born daughter.

But are we concerned about the ethics of fracking? Over 250 *billion* gallons of water have been permanently contaminated in the U.S., and the number increases by 25 million more gallons *every day*.

Is that the action of a pro-life lawmaker? A pro-life political party? A pro-life nation?

Leading pro-life activists are so concerned about the accidental loss of a fetus that an Alabama woman whose pregnancy was terminated by the five bullets an attacker fired at her faces years in prison for precipitating an "abortion" by starting the argument that led to the shooting.

Will there be any jail time for the fossil fuel CEOs and shareholders who have created a climate where wildfires tear through California towns and Greek villages and Israeli forests, killing hundreds?

Will there be manslaughter charges for the ship captains and train engineers and truck drivers who transport the oil and gas and coal killing both humans and members of countless other species in ferocious storms, devastating droughts, and cataclysmic floods?

Who goes to prison for widespread crop losses?

Who goes to prison for rising sea levels that cause billions in property damage and lead to higher death tolls from more frequent storm surges?

Pro-life voters are horrified by forced abortions in China and North Korea and the sterilization of nonconsenting women in the U.S. over many decades, while with a religious zeal we accept the forced destruction of our planet and most of the life on it, witnessing first-hand the 6th mass extinction event in planetary history.

Pro-life activists *say* they don't approve of radicals who have shot abortion clinic nurses, murdered abortion doctors in their churches, bombed abortion clinics. But their rhetoric insists that every avenue for stopping the slaughter of innocents must be pursued.

Will those of us who accept the reality of scientific findings be forced to target fossil fuel workers or CEOs or shareholders? Will we be forced to bomb oil tankers and storage facilities and wells?

If we do, can we claim self-defense? Those killing doctors insist they're saving the unborn. But if a pro-life activist can worry about a bean-sized clump of cells, why can't we worry about the billions of humans already here? Why can't we worry about the hundreds of trillions of other living beings?

Why can't we worry about the life that bean-sized clump of cells will face once forced into the world?

We're defending not only the unborn of all species but defending ourselves as well. We're the ones who die when the air quality in our major cities hits critical levels during weeks of wildfires. We're the ones who die in those wildfires, and in historic floods, and in ever-worsening heat waves. Over one hundred and ten thousand died in Europe and western Russia during the 2003 and 2010 heat waves. In June of 2019, France hit an all-time record high for any day ever—114.6 F.

And summer had barely begun.

CEOs of fossil fuel corporations aren't abortion "providers." They are abortion enforcers.

If pro-life activists are so concerned about the abortion of human fetuses that they'll back people like Donald Trump, how concerned are *we* about the crisis of climate abortion?

If those on the right are conflicted by the terrorist actions of their colleagues against abortion providers, those on the left who are even more pro-life are still more horrified. So what's someone who wants to stop the abortions forced on Mother Nature to do?

We must at the very least take action on a social and financial level. If churches can excommunicate members of their congregation who perform abortions, we can shun every oil field roughneck, every pipeline worker, every lawmaker who bans protests against fossil fuel companies, every fossil fuel secretary and salesperson, every fossil fuel CEO and shareholder.

We must petition our banks to stop funding pipelines and other fossil fuel infrastructure. We must change institutions if they won't.

We must demand our cities and universities divest from fossil fuels.

We can join climate strikes like the one scheduled for September 20.

If we are truly pro-life, if we want to remain a species Mother Earth won't *want* to abort, we must become the offspring that doesn't kill the moment we come out of the womb. Or the sequel to *It's Alive!* will be *We're All Goners!*

Relying on Ignorance, Poverty,
and Poor Health

Conservatives are afraid that if we give people "free" college, "free" healthcare, and "free" childcare, we'll make life too easy and people will lose every ounce of self-reliance they ever possessed. They'll have no "character" and become lazy, weak bums.

Of course, since conservatives already think the poor and working class are lazy and weak, I'm not exactly sure how much further they think we can slide. What's clear, though, is that denying us the things we need hasn't reformed our character in any meaningful way.

While right-wing pundits tremble at the thought of this "free" assistance, the rest of us understand perfectly that nothing is free. We understand that all government programs are paid for through taxes. We just prefer that our tax dollars go toward making the lives of people here in the U.S. better rather than using those funds to pay for endless wars abroad. And since we'll be relying on our own tax dollars to fund education and healthcare, that sounds kind of like self-reliance, anyway.

But even if it isn't, even if poor and working-class folks don't personally create every single advancement that improves their lives, I have to wonder just where exactly conservatives want to draw the line on self-reliance. My grandmother grew up without electricity. Her family had no indoor plumbing. They had no car, either walking where they wanted to go or taking a horse and wagon. They grew their own vegetables, milked their own cows, harvested their own popcorn.

They were certainly more self-reliant than most of the right-wing politicians worrying about the weak character of diabetics who can't afford their insulin, of children allergic to bee stings and peanuts who can't afford their EpiPens.

Does Mitch McConnell carry water half a mile from the creek to wash dishes or do laundry or bathe or drink? Does he spin his own cloth? Sew his own clothes?

Does Laura Ingraham string up her own hog and butcher it to put food on her table?

Does Paul Ryan can his own green beans? Make his own blackberry jam? Pickle his own cucumbers?

All summer and fall? Year after year after year?

If conservatives can still consider themselves decent human beings even with dishwashers and microwaves, the rest of us can be decent human beings with free public transportation and free childcare that allow us to hold down jobs so we can buy our own dishwashers and microwaves.

Conservatives say that providing education for every adult who wants it will create a nation of weaklings who can't support themselves. But I wonder if even they believe this illogical claim. Who among us feels *less* able to provide for ourselves because we've had a good education? Who among us feels *more* empowered to start a family when we graduate with $50,000 in student loan debt?

I wonder if maybe free courses in logic wouldn't benefit our country instead.

Perhaps *mandatory* courses in logic.

Most other industrialized nations have some form of these various "free" programs. I don't see Germany, Japan, and Sweden falling apart because their people have access to education and healthcare.

I'm not saying the underlying principle of self-reliance isn't a good thing. It is.

But so is cooperation. So is lifting people out of poverty. So is reducing ignorance. So is treating and healing the sick.

Has Sean Hannity installed the plumbing for every bathroom he's ever used? Has he personally constructed every house he's ever lived in? Dug every well for every glass of water he's been served?

If conservative leaders can't provide for their own basic needs and yet can still consider themselves morally competent, I'm not sure why allowing the rest of us to earn degrees and go to the dentist is going to turn America into a moral cesspool.

And really, who died and put them in charge of our character to begin with?

Americans don't need conservatives to worry about our moral fortitude. That is our responsibility. Of course, I can't deny that their own character might benefit from using their power and position to improve the lives of others rather than trying incessantly to "teach us a lesson." *That* kind of education they seem happy to provide for free.

As a society, we've already agreed that not only individuals but the nation as whole benefit from public funding for libraries, primary education, highways, fire departments, space exploration, and national parks.

Free healthcare, free secondary education, free childcare, free public transportation, and all the other things that will improve life for virtually everyone in the country are worthy of funding with taxpayer dollars as well.

Because a nation with millions of uneducated citizens living in poverty, and millions more living barely above it— unhappy, untrained, desperate people—isn't capable of self-reliance at all.

Death to the Liberals!

David Duke, as right-wing an ideologue as they come, approved of abortion—for blacks on welfare. Those of us on the left can leverage that kind of blind bigotry to further a liberal agenda.

Leftists, liberals, and progressives have different philosophies, and the labels mean different things to different people, but one thing is sure—conservatives want to eliminate all of us. Conservatives hate LGBTQ teachers "indoctrinating innocent children." The same goes for LGBTQ parents, for liberal and progressive and leftist parents teaching their own children.

Conservatives establish extreme gerrymandered boundaries for voting districts to reduce Democratic power. They disband and dismantle elected city governments run by Democrats and set up their own rulers in their place.

If conservatives hate us so much, let's angle their hatred to get concessions. They are free to keep abortion illegal for Republicans, but we can point out that if Democrats can get abortions, there will be fewer Democrats to worry about in the future.

Republicans can continue denying physician-assisted dying to their voters, but why not allow terminally ill Dems to check out a little sooner? It saves insurance companies money, always a plus for the party of business, but more importantly, it prevents older, wiser leftists from using those last six months to spew their nonsense. As stupid as liberals are, we *might* still be able to persuade one or two conservatives to our side before we go. We can point out that conservatives therefore benefit when progressives want Death with Dignity, as their opposition simply eliminate themselves without conservatives having to so much as threaten a Second Amendment remedy of any kind.

There's a growing movement to allow aid in dying for the non-terminally ill as well, those suffering chronic pain or untreatable depression. People in pain or despair make risky enemies. They have nothing to lose by radical forms of protest. We can show conservatives how to lessen that threat by letting idiot liberals kill themselves if they choose to.

At the very least, we can reason that each one of those dead liberals is a dead liberal voter.

The problem, of course, is that the benefits we're dangling to persuade conservatives to make these concessions are real benefits to conservative power. While having our pregnancies forcibly aborted or having someone else force us to take lethal drug combinations would be a form of cultural if not ethnic cleansing, the fact is that liberals, progressives, and leftists *do* want the legal options of making these choices for ourselves. Having the right to self-determination isn't the same as willingly walking into the gas chambers.

If we can persuade conservatives to make these concessions, liberals can then try to push society down the slippery slope that will be the only real reason conservatives would resist in the first place. Of course, if conservatives never want those freedoms and options for themselves, that's fine, too. Leftists are all about equal opportunities, but perhaps this time, we should worry just about our own and lobby for access to abortion and aid in dying for those the right-wing want out of their lives anyway. We can make this a win/win scenario.

Boxers, wrestlers, and military commanders always try to leverage their opponents' weaknesses to their benefit. So let's use the hatred and disdain conservatives feel for us to our advantage. Their fear and animosity can be our salvation. To gain the autonomy we want over our own lives, let's boldly campaign for death—the death of at least these three forms of oppression.

Dinosaurs Building the World's Largest Magnet

When we look back at the tragic end of the Age of Dinosaurs, we assume they were helpless victims of natural forces. But what if the dinosaurs brought their deaths upon themselves?

Humans boast of being the most intelligent species this planet has ever known. Understanding the cataclysmic event that wiped out the dinosaurs 65 million years ago, we make modest efforts to prepare for another large asteroid heading our way. We entertain ourselves with movies about destroying those dangerous objects before they strike the Earth, showing ourselves superior to those lumbering creatures who didn't know what hit them.

All the while actively seeking self-destruction.

We "harvest" our forests "sustainably," even though any seedling planted today will require two hundred years or more to reach the size of the tree being replaced. And that's in industrialized nations. In Brazil, the Amazon rainforest is being cut down faster than anyone can replant it, not even to harvest the wood but just to clear the land. Fires are deliberately set to clear even more. And the climate crisis has led to record numbers of "natural" wildfires—over 70,000—raging across the area, destroying one of the world's largest carbon sinks even more rapidly.

We cut down indigenous forests in southeast Asia to make way for palm oil plantations.

We tear up regulations that would help prevent the extinction of endangered species, even knowing we're in the midst of a global mass extinction event.

We create and incorporate per- and polyfluoroalkyl substances (PFAS), even knowing they contaminate drinking water everywhere they're used. We continue to use pesticides that are not only linked to cancer but also wipe out bee populations, even knowing that bees are the sole pollinators for many plants essential to human welfare.

We develop nuclear weapons and cancel nuclear arms treaties. We develop biological and chemical weapons designed to kill millions of people at a time (and virtually every other lifeform living among them). We continue operating nuclear power plants, despite the evidence they aren't safe from nature, much less from human fallibility and malevolence.

We refuse to end our dependence on fossils fuels, drilling new wells every day, fighting any legislation to curb our fossil fuel use, criminalizing protests by those who don't want to end up like the dinosaurs.

But because we keep adding more carbon to the atmosphere as quickly as we can, fully knowing the devastation it causes, we are active participants in our own self-destruction. We watch as Greenland's ice sheet melts faster than predicted. We watch as the ice in Antarctica melts. We watch as record heat waves kill hundreds of people, thousands, tens of thousands.

We watch as large corporations legally steal water around the world. Fracking, of course, continues unabated, permanently contaminating hundreds of millions more gallons of groundwater every day.

We brush off the few political candidates who recognize the crisis and want to do something about it. We criticize and insult and lambast our friends who want to support those candidates.

It's like watching the most intelligent species of dinosaur develop the world's biggest magnet and point it toward the asteroid belt, deliberately attracting the largest iron-nickel objects they can find, boasting that they are about to create incredible new opportunities with all the precious metals they're bringing to the Earth.

Keeping the Pantry Full: Justice, Freedom, and Equality Don't Have Fairy Tale Endings

"I can't wait till the Mueller report comes out." "I can't wait until the mid-term elections." "I can't wait till we elect a new president in 2020." Almost everyone I know is working hard to get us out of the terrible political predicament we're currently in, but only a handful seem to recognize that none of these things is a permanent fix. Justice, freedom, and equality don't have fairy tale endings. There's no moment after which we can live happily ever after. Maintaining freedom and justice and equality will be a constant battle, not only in our lifetimes but forever.

Have we ever heard someone say, "I finally got all the weeds out of my yard. I never have to worry about that again"?

Have we heard anyone say, "Whew. I'm finally down to my ideal weight and BMI. Now I can stop exercising and watching what I eat"?

Or "I finally have the right to marry, and I've married the man of my dreams. It's all coasting from here"?

Whatever our personal end goals are for "progress," whether that be electing anyone other than Trump, or trying to get Democrats to move to the left, or to implement full-fledged socialism, Election Day is not the end of the struggle. The "Revolution" is not the end.

The work we do is hard. We want it to be over. We want to "win" and finally have a chance to breathe, but the painful truth is we can never relax.

Critics of reform point out that reforms can always be undone. That's true. But revolution and complete overhaul can be undone, too. The people's revolution in Russia didn't bring about lasting change. Within a decade, socialism had been corrupted into communism. Before long, Russia and then the Soviet Union were oppressive tyrannies.

Everything can be undone. That doesn't mean we shouldn't push Dems to the left, that we shouldn't try to shift to Democratic Socialism, that we shouldn't bring about Trotsky socialism. It just means that whatever path we choose, we must realize our end goals are no more secure than anyone else's. Your system may be better than my system, but it's every bit as susceptible to failure as any other.

That's because human beings will be working each and every type of system we ever develop, and no humans of any persuasion are perfect. It seems a trite and obvious point, but every day I see people who think that if they get *their* way, if *their* idea of the perfect candidate or perfect policy or perfect economic or political system is victorious, we'll finally be okay.

We can be better, but we'll never be okay.

Again, that doesn't mean we should fall into cynicism or despair. We just need to have realistic expectations.

Protecting and preserving something great is a never-ending battle. Religious fanatics in the past decade have destroyed Persian artifacts dating back nearly 2000 years. Catholic invaders 500 years ago destroyed every Mayan book they could find. Thousands of temples, churches, synagogues, and mosques around the world, some of them hundreds of years old, have been destroyed over the years by enemies of the worshippers who met there.

We can preserve national parks against predators (you know, coal and oil companies, loggers, off-road recreational vehicles) every day for decades and decades, but all that work can be undone overnight once one of those predators finally gets in.

Holocaust survivors are murdered 70 years after their liberation from the camps.

There will *never* be a time when we can let our guard down.

Why in the world would we expect something different in the political and economic world? Because *those* things are simpler, smaller, and easier to control?

We must fight to make the world a better place, but we must do so with the understanding that such an endeavor requires a permanent commitment. Every advance we achieve must be supervised and monitored. We must always maintain oversight. We must continually keep pressure on all involved to preserve each and every victory.

We just returned from the dentist with clean teeth and a clean bill of health, with no cavities or gum disease? That's great, but we'd better keep brushing and flossing.

Folks in AA take things "one day at a time." They understand a universal truth, that one must always maintain constant vigilance, that even thirty or forty years of sobriety can be lost with a single night of drinking.

We just got back from the grocery and filled our fridge? Would any of us ever consider that a *final* victory?

Anyway, you get the point. I need to conclude now. It's time for semi-annual maintenance sex with my husband. He seems reluctant to head into the bedroom with me, but I really don't understand why. I bathed last month, didn't I? I'm good.

Who Will You Hide and Who Will Hide You?

When Kellyanne Conway was asked a question about President Trump's latest racist remarks, she demanded the reporter answer her own question before responding. "What is your ethnicity?" she asked imperiously, threateningly.

We've reached the moment that Miep Gies once faced. Will we hide Otto Frank and his family or will we let them be carted away to the camps?

When I converted to Judaism in the mid-1990s, my rabbi asked me, "Are you willing to face another Holocaust if it comes to that?"

It was a question I'd already considered for twenty years. In my Baptist high school in Metairie, just a mile from KKK leader David Duke's home, we'd watched *The Hiding Place*, about Dutch Christians sent to the camps for hiding Jews. As a teenage Mormon priest, I talked with a young man from a neighboring congregation who'd just returned from his mission in Argentina, where he'd been kidnapped and tortured. As a missionary myself in Rome, my mission president warned us of a threat to kidnap two missionaries in Italy and force them to confess to being CIA agents.

When I came out as gay, I read *The Pink Triangle* and other books about gay men who were sent to concentration and death camps along with Jews, Jehovah's Witnesses, and political dissidents. Upon coming out, I wrote letters to the editor of my New Orleans newspaper. I wrote to my senators and representatives. I wrote to Church leaders in Salt Lake. I wanted to make sure I was on someone's list, so if things "ever got bad," I'd know I couldn't "pass" but would have to fight.

So I was ready for my rabbi's question. "Yes," I said. "I'm prepared."

He smiled back at me. "You won't have to face such a thing here," he said. "This is America."

I was surprised, expecting him to understand human nature better than that. By that point, I'd already lost a friend to gay bashing. Only a few years later, after I relocated to Seattle in the aftermath of Hurricane Katrina, six women were shot at the Jewish Federation in Belltown, one fatally. I never went to synagogue without looking for two or three ways out.

Years later, after I was no longer Jewish or Mormon but atheist, I attended a birthday party in my Rainier Beach neighborhood. A woman who struck up a conversation with me mentioned that her husband was a builder. "My father was a contractor," I told her in return. Then I added, as an afterthought, "I even designed a house for him to build me one day that had a secret room so I could hide Jews if I needed to."

She stared at me a moment before replying. "Thank you." It turned out she was Jewish, and she'd had this discussion growing up. Who did she know, her parents asked, who might hide her?

Just as many black parents have a talk with their children about what to do if they are ever stopped by the police, several gay people I knew had had talks with their families about who might hide them if gays were ever rounded up. My Mormon aunt and uncle promised to hide me.

Of course, they're no longer speaking to me, so I guess that escape route is gone.

The president of the United States is a racist. So are many of his followers. The evidence is so overwhelming it doesn't even need analysis anymore.

The other day, I saw cell phone video of several people forming a human chain to keep ICE agents from arresting one of their neighbors. The neighbors faced arrest themselves, perhaps beating or tasing.

How long will it be before good people trying to protect other good people are shot for doing so?

Who will you hide, when officials come for the Latinos and Muslims and Jews and blacks in your life? It's a discussion with our friends and family we can't put off any longer.

But it's not the only question we need to ask during those discussions. We also need to ask who will be willing to hide us when the government comes for "treasonous" dissenters and protesters. Who will hide us when agents come for "lying" journalists, "race traitors," and "gender traitors"?

Maria von Trapp and her family didn't climb over the Alps to escape Nazi occupation of Austria. They drove out a day before the borders were closed.

While we're having these life and death discussions with our families and friends, we'd better make sure our passports are in order as well.

Don't Let This Happen to You

I've had sex with hundreds of men over the years and had quite a bit of fun. I was reasonably hot, looked good in leather, and could get a stranger to approach me for sex almost any time I sat out on my front stoop.

That's not the case anymore.

I'm no longer a trim 145 pounds but a monstrous 221. But it wasn't the 221st pound that was the problem. It was the 146th.

Knowing that a person's weight fluctuates a few pounds back and forth regularly, I wasn't worried when the scale told me I weighed 146. The pendulum would swing back the other way in a day or two. No biggie.

But it didn't. A couple of days later, the scale let me know I'd gained yet another pound.

I shrugged. 147 was still quite a desirable weight. My clothes still fit. Men still asked me to unzip for them. No need to go into a panic.

Before long, 147 was my norm, and when I went up to 148, I figured my weight would go back down in another couple of days to that new normal.

It didn't.

Little by little, I gained "a pound." And one day after waking up to discover I weighed 180 pounds, I finally realized I was in serious trouble. I had to do something about the situation immediately. I decreased my calorie intake, increased my exercise, and over the next four or five months, I worked my way back to 175.

It was exhausting. So I decided to take a short break.

And somehow, by increasing my weight a pound here and a pound there, I eventually found myself reaching 190. At that point, I felt so overwhelmed at the task ahead of me that I kept putting off a full assault on the fat until I had more time and energy and dedication.

Then my weight edged up to 210. And kept going.

Guys don't want to have sex with me anymore. Not even my husband. And who can blame them? I see myself in the mirror every day, and that's horrific enough, but when I see a photograph, I gasp. Do I really look that bad?

The last time I had my picture taken for my driver's license, the employee who took the photo showed me the result and asked sadly, "You want to try that again?"

"There's no point," I told him. "That's what I look like." His expression of pity was hard to take, but I smiled and went on my way.

I don't get looks of pity anymore. I get noses turned up in disgust. If I'm lucky, people pretend they don't see me at all. A toothless homeless man offered to give me a blow job the other day, and I almost took him up on it, knowing he probably had as much trouble finding a willing sex partner as I did.

I'm only 58. My sex life shouldn't be over already. I feel like I've lost a lower leg but still experience phantom pain. I want my leg back so I can treat the pain.

A couple of months ago, I flirted with a man I saw regularly on my daily commute, and finally I gave him my phone number. I was thrilled when he gave me a call, and even more thrilled when he came over to the house. My husband graciously offered to run errands for a couple of hours. Maybe this reward would give me the encouragement to face the gargantuan task of losing weight.

The sex was awful. The new guy was hot, mind you, and quite skilled. The problem was me. Somehow, as I got fatter, my dick got shorter. I never had an Olympic-sized penis to begin with, but I sported a respectable five and three-quarter inches. (Men are like children who say, "I'm four and a half years old." That "half" is important to them.)

Fully erect, I now measure just under three inches.

Three inches!

I was mortified, even more so when I couldn't get far enough past my new friend's buttocks to enter him. Our tryst went downhill from there. You can be sure he never called again.

I asked my doctor for ED pills, and I invested in a cock ring, but neither of those addressed the underlying problem—obesity. I struggle to buckle my belt. I can't even see my penis when I urinate.

Why did I let my weight get so out of control? The mere thought of losing 75 pounds is enough to depress me into contemplating a foolish ice cream purchase.

But I can't eat ice cream because I'm now diabetic. And yet even avoiding carbs (for the most part, anyway) and walking more, I haven't lost a single pound. Then that gets me so discouraged I wonder if I'll be able to stabilize at 221 and stop further deterioration into an even more horrific creature.

Of course, sex and health aren't the only two issues with being fat. When I go for a job interview, I watch the interviewers pretend they aren't recoiling as I walk into the room. Employers treat you differently, and coworkers, and complete strangers. Friends treat you differently as well. Maybe not all of them, but quite a few. And making new friends becomes much more difficult. I work in customer service and try to be friendly and efficient, maybe a little funny, but I recognize the moment the person in front of me begins thinking I'm a troll coming on to them. The mixture of worry and repulsion on their faces is like a knife to the heart.

If only that knife could be redirected to perform a gastric bypass. But my insurance won't cover the procedure.

I'm too ashamed of my weight to eat in public. I imagine people watching me and thinking, "He doesn't need that scoop of mashed potatoes." I clearly do eat too much, and I suppose it's an addiction or mental illness of some sort. I don't think it's just "moral weakness," though there may be some of that thrown in, too. It's been a lifelong struggle, and there's no way to hide my shame. I can't "pass" as a normal person. Everyone can see at a glance that I have no "self-control."

My husband insists we eat dinner together. I've read articles about the importance of shared meals, so I consent, but my husband will often just stare at my plate or stare at me while I eat. At least, I *feel* like he's staring. Whatever he may or may not be thinking, it *feels* like judgment. And there are plenty of times when he says, "You're having a second serving?" in an incredulous tone. My second serving may be small, but it's a second serving. He may have a snack himself an hour later, and maybe another snack an hour after that. But he's not big, so there's no moral condemnation for him.

For fat people, there is always a double standard to go with our double servings. And we're judged the moment we take the first bite of the first serving. I've heard enough comments from enough people to know that it's not all in my head. How do you enjoy a meal when you are judged every single second you're at the table? It's psychologically devastating.

And yet there are moments I can forget, when I can have normal conversations, joke and laugh, talk with coworkers about better ways to serve our customers, talk with friends about movies or what we can do to make a positive difference in the world.

I volunteered as a Mormon missionary for two years as a young adult. I worked as a gay activist after that. I now advocate for single-payer healthcare and tuition-free college and guaranteed childcare. I'm all about "spreading the word." But if a newspaper publishes one of my op-eds and includes a current photo of my fat face, my words are immediately devalued. Who can trust someone's assessment of grand issues who is incapable of dealing with his own individual problems?

I see 25-year-olds and 30-year-olds at work or on the bus or at the store, guys just five or six or ten pounds overweight. I have to stop myself from approaching them and saying, "Nip this in the bud!" They'd just think I was a freak.

I'm left with little more than one viable option for passing on my "wisdom": a T-shirt—size XXL, of course—with "Don't let this happen to you!" emblazoned on the front, and the warning, "It's that first extra pound you have to worry about" on my back.

I've been fat, and I've been thin, and I can assure those of you who aren't concerned about being a few pounds overweight that you probably should be. I applaud activists fighting against fat shaming, but even among friends who are accepting and non-judgmental, life is better in almost every way possible when you're fit.

I may not have much wisdom to impart, but please take my word for it—it's that *first* extra pound you need to worry about if you don't want to carry an extra seventy pounds with you everywhere you go for the rest of your life. You don't need any fad diets or radical programs or compulsive behavior to lose one single pound. So just make sure you never need to lose more than that.

Sixteen ounces of prevention is worth seventy pounds of cure. And that's a bargain in anyone's calorie account.

The Climate Crisis Is World War III

World War I left 20 million people dead across the globe, more than half of them civilians. World War II killed between 70 and 85 million more, 3% of the world's population. Between 50 and 55 million of those deaths were civilians.

What kind of death toll lies ahead if there is ever a World War III?

We'll find out soon enough, as the third world war is already underway.

A Planet Called Treason was my first Orson Scott Card novel. I loved how the title offered the reader multiple meanings. On the one hand, the planet in question is named Treason, like our planet is named Terra. But Card, a devout Mormon, provided his planet with a spirit, the way Mormon theology insists the Earth has a spirit of its own, separate from the spirits inhabiting all the various life forms on and below its surface. When the planet in the novel is betrayed by the actions of its villains, the planet calls out "Treason!" through the way it reacts.

Most of the wars in mankind's past have pitted humans against each other. But now humans have declared war on the planet itself. It isn't fighting back, as in Card's novel, so much as allowing its attackers to shoot themselves in the foot and step on their own land mines.

In Michael Moore's documentary *Fahrenheit 11/9*, we see a clip of a young Asian woman concentrating on her phone. "'This is not a drill,'" she reads the text alert she's just received. "Oh, my god!" She looks at her partner in stunned confusion. "What do we do?"

For twenty minutes on January 13, 2018, the people of Hawaii desperately tried to reach their loved ones as they mistakenly believed they faced almost certain death from an incoming nuclear missile. In our current political climate, the threat of a devastating global war, which had mostly lain dormant since the end of the Cold War, now hangs over our heads once again.

The last world war was so catastrophic that we've repeatedly tried to imagine what World War III would look like. Movies such as *The Day After*, *Red Dawn*, *Dr. Strangelove*, and *War Games* helped us prepare to survive or prevent such a calamity.

But despite all the forethought, we were still blindsided.

The climate crisis is a far larger threat than the Kaiser ever was, a more dangerous threat than the Nazis could ever dream of being, a more powerful threat than the Soviet Union or China or any other political or military entity. We can rebuild Berlin or Hiroshima or Beirut or Atlanta.

We can't rebuild an entire planet.

In the coming decades, almost 600 coastal cities around the world, housing an estimated 800 million people, will face permanent inundation or repeated heavy storm surges from increasingly severe hurricanes and cyclones.

That's just the damage along the coastlines.

The Vietnam War lasted two decades. The War of the Roses last thirty-two years. The Spanish conquest of the Inca Empire took place over forty years. The Hundred Years' War actually dragged on for 116 years. The *second* Hundred Years' War lasted 126.

The cost of rebuilding or relocating homes, businesses, factories, farms, and people during World War III will likely dwarf spending from all previous wars combined. Right-wing conservatives will look back with nostalgia to the times when immigrants and refugees only numbered in the low millions. Ancient, deadly pathogens released from the ice or permafrost will almost certainly contribute to even further suffering.

Anne Frank wasn't officially executed during World War II. She died of disease that proliferated because of conditions created during the war.

Terra isn't going to die. Probably 10-15% of the species still alive today will survive as well. And not all deaths during a conflict happen at the beginning.

That doesn't mean we aren't at war right now.

The gas chambers we're being led to today are filled with a gas just as deadly as the hydrogen cyanide-based gas used during the Holocaust. Just as deadly as the mustard gas used in the first world war.

We've thought about World War III for 75 years, but we don't have to wonder if or when it will begin any longer. The only relevant question now is how we're going to win this ultimate War of the World.

And whether we'll ever be lucky enough to face World War IV.

Eat, Drink, Be Merry, and Work for Justice

In our endless fight for justice and equality, we often forget to take time to live, which leads to psychological overload. Some people end up turning off the news for weeks at a time because they can't bear to hear one more horrible thing. But even without the news, they're already so emotionally exhausted they can barely manage a pleasant conversation over a comforting meal. A friend of mine forced herself to watch Mueller testify for hours, saying, "I want to turn it off but—just like I always feel about the news—I think it's irresponsible to look away during such a depressing time in our history." We need to seek a balance that allows us the chance to enjoy life while accepting our responsibility to make things better.

During times when I've struggled financially, my friend Paul sent me $20 in an envelope filled with movie reviews and other articles he thinks will interest me. He told me he was willing to send the money every couple of weeks under one condition—that I not use it on anything mundane like paying bills but instead use it to treat myself. I was to report back on how I spent the money, as hearing the report would give him pleasure as well.

So I'd buy a DVD of *Safety Not Guaranteed* or *I, Robot*. I'd order a Margherita pizza at Tutta Bella, which would transport me back to my days in Napoli. I'd splurge on a couple of jars of delicious and low-calorie pickled okra.

I spend a lot of my free time writing op-eds that I hope will help persuade people to change harmful opinions and actions on a variety of subjects. I also write to give encouragement to those already doing more than I am on these issues, especially in the increasingly urgent battle to address the climate crisis. But my husband does far more, spending ten to fifteen hours a week in classes and discussion groups and executive meetings. He protests at rallies. He hands out flyers. He goes door to door selling subscriptions to the *Freedom Socialist* newspaper, despite it triggering odious memories of his time as Mormon missionary.

But we're not miserable. Well, sometimes we are. We're human, after all. But we make sure even on our busiest days to do something fun together. We watch reruns of *The Big Bang Theory.* I can watch the friends play "Emily or Cinnamon?" over and over. I never get tired of watching Amy's reaction when Sheldon suggests they have a long-distance relationship if his application to live on Mars is accepted.

We watch *Mom.* We watch Germany's *Crime Scene Cleaner*, about a man who cleans up murder and suicide scenes. It's a comedy, and yes, it's funny.

Most of the fun my husband and I have is on the cheap side, since we can't afford things like trips to New York or Tokyo, but even people with limited means can find ways to keep their spirits up at least a little. We take walks together when we can. We go window shopping at hardware stores. We participate in a book club. We share funny memes.

Since maintaining a mental safe zone for ourselves is essential, whether we're working on important social and environmental issues or not, we must tailor our mental health activities to our individual tastes. If we're partnered or part of a large family, sometimes that means doing things together and sometimes it means doing things by ourselves.

One of my friends gets energized watching superhero movies. Another friend enjoys biking and taking pictures of trains. Yet another likes Moth radio. I like listening to Maroon 5 and Pink.

In this critical moment, we *must* be activists on some level, but we aren't obliged to be miserable. In fact, we're of little use if we allow ourselves to burn out.

Let's work for justice to the best of our abilities, but let's eat, drink, and be as merry as life allows while doing it.

About the Author

Johnny Townsend earned an MFA in fiction writing from Louisiana State University. He was also awarded a BA and MA in English, as well as a BS in Biology. A native of New Orleans, Townsend relocated to Seattle in the aftermath of Hurricane Katrina. After attending a Baptist high school for four years as a teenager, he volunteered as a Mormon missionary in Italy and then held positions in his local New Orleans ward as Second Counselor in the Elders Quorum, Ward Single Adult Representative, Stake Single Adult Chair, Sunday School Teacher, Stake Missionary, and Ward Membership Clerk. In the secular world, Townsend worked as a book store clerk, a college English instructor, a bank teller, a loan processor, a mail carrier, a library associate, a receptionist, and a professional escort. He worked selling bus passes, installing insulation, delivering pizza, cleaning residential construction sites, rehabilitating developmentally disabled adults, surveying gas stations, translating documents from Italian into English, preparing surgical carts for medical teams, and performing experiments on rat brains in a physiology lab.

Townsend has published stories and essays in *Newsday*, *The Washington Post*, *The Los Angeles Times*, *The Salt Lake Tribune*, *The Orlando Sentinel*, *The Army Times*, *The Humanist*, *The Progressive*, *Medical Reform*, *Christopher Street*, *The Massachusetts Review*, *Glimmer Train*, *Sunstone*,

Dialogue: A Journal of Mormon Thought, in the anthologies *Queer Fish, Off the Rocks, Moth and Rust, The Kindness of Strangers,* and *In Our Lovely Deseret: Mormon Fictions.* He helped edit *Latter-Gay Saints,* a collection of stories about gay Mormons, and he is the author of 38 books.

Most of those books are collections of Mormon short stories, and several have been named to Kirkus Reviews' Best of 2011, 2012, 2013, 2014, and 2015. In addition to his Mormon stories, Townsend has written a collection of Jewish stories, *The Golem of Rabbi Loew,* based on his years as a Jew. He has also written one non-fiction book, *Let the Faggots Burn: The UpStairs Lounge Fire,* having interviewed survivors as well as friends and relatives of the 32 people who were killed when an arsonist set fire to a gay bar in the French Quarter of New Orleans on Gay Pride Day in 1973. He is an Associate Producer of the feature-length documentary *Upstairs Inferno,* directed by Robert Camina.

Townsend sang in the New Orleans Gay Men's Chorus for a time and performed in the priests' chorus in the opera *Aida.* He has a collection of Victorian ceramic tiles, wooden dinosaur carvings from Bali, and the entire set of Calvin and Hobbes comic strip compilations in Italian. In addition to speaking English and Italian, he's also studied French, Spanish, Russian, Hebrew, Old English, and American Sign Language. Townsend is an avid movie fan, whose three favorite Hitchcock films are *Shadow of a Doubt, Strangers on a Train,* and *Rear Window.* He gives regularly to environmental conservation groups, medical charities, groups that support single-payer healthcare, human rights organizations, and to various documentaries and other projects he finds on crowdfunding sites.

The University of Utah in Salt Lake City has a Special Collection of Townsend material, including all his books, the magazines and newspapers that have published his work, his journals, his correspondence, photographs, and even a portrait painted by a prominent gay artist. ONE Archives in Los Angeles, the national gay and lesbian archive, has his UpStairs Lounge materials and his 20 original gay quilts.

Johnny Townsend is married to Gary Tolman, another former Mormon who worked in the same mission in Italy. They still speak Italian to each other regularly.

Books by Johnny Townsend

Thanks for reading! If you enjoyed this book, could you please take a few minutes to write a review online? Reviews are helpful both to me as an author and to other readers, so we'd all sincerely appreciate your writing one! And if you did enjoy the book, here are some others I've written you might want to look up:

Mormon Underwear

God's Gargoyles

The Circumcision of God

Sex among the Saints

Dinosaur Perversions

Zombies for Jesus

The Abominable Gayman

The Gay Mormon Quilter's Club

The Golem of Rabbi Loew

Mormon Fairy Tales

Flying over Babel

Marginal Mormons

Mormon Bullies

The Mormon Victorian Society

Dragons of the Book of Mormon

Selling the City of Enoch

A Day at the Temple

Behind the Zion Curtain

Gayrabian Nights

Lying for the Lord

Despots of Deseret

Missionaries Make the Best Companions

Invasion of the Spirit Snatchers

The Tyranny of Silence

Sex on the Sabbath

The Washing of Brains

The Mormon Inquisition

Interview with a Mission President

Weeping, Wailing, and Gnashing of Teeth

Behind the Bishop's Door

The Moat around Zion

The Last Days Linger

Mormon Madness

Human Compassion for Beginners

Dead Mankind Walking

Who Invited You to the Orgy?

Breaking the Promise of the Promised Land

Let the Faggots Burn: The UpStairs Lounge Fire

Latter-Gay Saints: An Anthology of Gay Mormon Fiction (co-editor)

Available from BookLocker.com or your favorite online or neighborhood bookstore.

Wondering what some of those other books are about? Read on!

The Washing of Brains

A world-weary man becomes a widower for the third time. A non-Mormon couple allow their teenage daughter to be baptized but are then shocked when she rejects them and moves in with a more righteous family. A man awakens to celebrate a milestone birthday only to discover that horrifying world events demand his attention instead. A budding feminist tries to make a political statement by giving birth to her "illegitimate" son in church just before Mother's Day. Missionaries in Rome try to prevent a terrorist bombing. The Prophet devises a plan to reverse global warming. A Salt Lake bishop is overwhelmed by his congregants' secrets. A gay Mormon man devastated by the breakup of his marriage to a closeted Hasidic Jew considers returning to the fold. An unhappy bartender reminisces about the affair he had with his mission president in Paris. A returned missionary takes a job in an adult video store. A young woman befriends the dungeon master who lives above her. A BYU student working as an escort finds love.

Invasion of the Spirit Snatchers

During the Apocalypse, a group of Mormon survivors in Hurricane, Utah gather in the home of the Relief Society president, telling stories to pass the time as they ration their food storage and await the Second Coming. But this is no ordinary group of Mormons—or perhaps it is. They are the faithful, feminist, gay, apostate, and repentant, all working together to help each other through the darkest days any of them have yet seen.

Gayrabian Nights

Gayrabian Nights is a twist on the well-known classic, *1001 Arabian Nights*, in which Scheherazade, under the threat of death if she ceases to captivate

King Shahryar's attention, enchants him through a series of mysterious, adventurous, and romantic tales.

In this variation, a male escort, invited to the hotel room of a closeted, homophobic Mormon senator, learns that the man is poised to vote on a piece of anti-gay legislation the following morning. To prevent him from sleeping, so that the exhausted senator will miss casting his vote on the Senate floor, the escort entertains him with stories of homophobia, celibacy, mixed orientation marriages, reparative therapy, coming out, first love, gay marriage, and long-term successful gay relationships. The escort crafts the stories to give the senator a crash course in gay culture and sensibilities, hoping to bring the man closer to accepting his own sexual orientation.

Let the Faggots Burn: The UpStairs Lounge Fire

On Gay Pride Day in 1973, someone set the entrance to a French Quarter gay bar on fire. In the terrible inferno that followed, thirty-two people lost their lives, including a third of the local congregation of the Metropolitan Community Church, their pastor burning to death halfway out a second-story window as he tried to claw his way to freedom. A mother who'd gone to the bar with her two gay sons died alongside them. A man who'd helped his friend escape first was found dead near the fire escape. Two children waited outside a movie theater across town for a father and step-father who would never pick them up. During this era of rampant homophobia, several families refused to claim the bodies, and many churches refused to bury the dead. Author Johnny Townsend pored through old records and tracked down survivors of the fire as well as relatives and friends of those killed to compile this fascinating account of a forgotten moment in gay history.

The Abominable Gayman

What is a gay Mormon missionary doing in Italy? He is trying to save his own soul as well as the souls of others. In these tales chronicling the two-year mission of Robert Anderson, we see a young man tormented by his inability to be the man the Church says he should be. In addition to his personal hell,

Anderson faces a major earthquake, organized crime, a serious bus accident, and much more. He copes with horrendous mission leaders and his own suicidal tendencies. But one day, he meets another missionary who loves him, and his world changes forever.

Marginal Mormons

What happens when a High Priest becomes addicted to crack cocaine? Should an unemployed bank teller take in a homeless protester from the Occupy movement? Do gay people have positive near-death experiences or unhappy ones? Is there a way to splice the empathy gene into the genome of every human? Can a schizophrenic woman on anti-delusional drugs still keep her belief in an intangible God? Will a childless biochemist be able to find fulfillment by taking part in a mission to Mars? Should a stay-at-home mom become involved in an international protest against fracking? Not every Latter-day Saint has a mainstream story to tell, but these soul-searching people are still more than the marginal Mormons headquarters would like us to believe.

Despots of Deseret

In this collection of Mormon short stories, a man learns to forgive his mother for an unspeakable atrocity. An uncle awaits word on his niece caught up in the 2004 tsunami. A bereaved man receives an unexpected gift from his deceased husband on Valentine's Day. A stake president threatens to revoke a couple's temple marriage. An elderly woman breaks her hip and struggles desperately to reach the phone. A young woman faces a shocking tragedy while serving as a missionary in Paraguay. A Mormon teenager wants to be named Best Christian Example at his Baptist high school. Conflict over finances arises in an interracial marriage. An anti-Mormon mob threatens a church outing. A virginal gay man takes out a contract on his own life to protect his virtue.

Sex among the Saints

Clean-cut Mormons may preach purity and wholesomeness, but sometimes repressing sexual instincts forces those feelings to erupt in unexpected ways. Here, two young women vie for the sexual affections of the same missionary. An elderly farmer marries his best friend's mistress in order to feel closer to both of them. A woman is dumped by the husband who gave her HIV. A missionary who posed for a shirtless calendar is kidnapped by his former girlfriend and forced into intercourse. A woman fantasizes about her sex life as one of Jesus' future wives. These tales are not for those who deny the reality of sexuality, but the rest of us will enjoy getting a glimpse into the Mormon bedroom.

Missionaries Make the Best Companions

What lies behind the freshly scrubbed façades of the Mormon missionaries we see about town? In these stories, an ex-Mormon tries to seduce a faithful elder by showing him increasingly suggestive movies. A sister missionary fulfills her community service requirement by babysitting for a prostitute. Two elders break their mission rules by venturing into the forbidden French Quarter. A black Mormon deals with racism in the Church. A senior missionary couple try to reactivate lapsed members while their own family falls apart back home. A young man hopes that serving a second full-time mission will lead him up the Church hierarchy. Two bored missionaries decide to make a little extra money moonlighting in a male stripper club. Two frustrated elders find an acceptable way to masturbate—by donating to a Fertility Clinic. A lonely man searches for the favorite companion he hasn't seen in thirty years.

Dragons of the Book of Mormon

A supporter of Prop 8 is forced to attend his boss's gay wedding. A devout Latter-day Saint struggling to pay his bills wonders if he should keep paying tithing, even after being excommunicated. A reporter seeks the identity of Salt Lake's new superhero—a masked man wearing temple clothes who mysteriously shows up at crime scenes. A woman is murdered in the temple on her wedding day. A devoted husband loses his wife on their wedding anniversary. One of the Three Nephites is missing in Pasadena. Mormons survive the zombie apocalypse because of their two-year supply of food storage.

Mormon Underwear

Mormon Underwear tells the stories of gay Mormons that mainstream members don't want to hear. Whether it is a young LDS man stripping to his Mormon underwear in public or a virginal 70-year-old finally giving in to temptation, a straight son who discovers his father kissing another man or a group who plots to put gays into positions of power within the Church, these are the stories too shameful or shocking to be told among traditional Saints.

The Golem of Rabbi Loew

Jacob and Esau Cohen are the closest of brothers. In fact, they're lovers. A doctor tries to combine canine genes with those of Jews, to improve their chances of surviving a hostile world. A Talmudic scholar dates an escort. A scientist tries to develop the "God spot" in the brains of his patients in order to create a messiah. The Golem of Prague is really Rabbi Loew's secret lover. While some of the Jews in Townsend's book are Orthodox, this collection of Jewish stories most certainly is not.

God's Gargoyles

These thirteen tales of gay Mormons reveal abominable yet delightful secrets. A man obsessed with gargoyles battles his own subhuman attitudes on Halloween. A gay couple steals from the rich to provide for their favorite charities. A celibate 38-year-old dates a promiscuous porn reviewer. A schizophrenic man accustomed to hearing voices suddenly starts to receive real revelations. There are as many gay Mormon stories to tell as there as gay Mormons, and this collection gives us just a taste of the rich narrative source this unique segment of Mormonism offers.

Mormon Fairy Tales

In these stories, we discover how the Three Nephites from the Book of Mormon cope with their frustrated sexuality when their wives aren't immortal as they are. A deceased sinner plots to break out of Spirit Prison. An obsessive-compulsive missionary covers himself with sacred protective garments. A polygamist in 1855 Utah is ordered to take a fourth wife, when all he really wants is to be with another man. A mentally unstable woman abandoned by the Church is driven to homelessness. A disappointed wife plots revenge when her temple worker husband sues the Church for an on-the-job injury. Aliens visiting the UN reveal that God really does live on a planet orbiting Kolob. In his tenth book, Johnny Townsend shows us yet again why he is "an important voice in the Mormon community."

The Mormon Victorian Society

A Victorian enthusiast has a startling sexual revelation to make at his monthly Society meeting. A father tries desperately to save his family from the imminent danger of global warming. Two men find love in the aftermath of Hurricane Katrina. A gay man attending his first Affirmation conference becomes embroiled in ex-Mormon politics. A home teaching assignment goes terribly wrong when a man whose father was murdered in a gay bar is confronted with a young gay cowboy. A Relief Society president is trapped on a plane next to a gay man flaunting his sexuality. A ministering angel to a young god tires of his position. Gay Mormons react when the Prophet has a new revelation about homosexuality.

Lying for the Lord

In this collection of Mormon short stories, a missionary in Italy makes a break for freedom on Christmas. A youth outing for priests at a shooting range doesn't go as planned. Mormons create a theocracy in America and rename the country Zion. An unhappy sister missionary in New Orleans ponders just what her calling to serve really entails. A conflicted father wonders how to deal with a transgender son who wants to be his daughter. A white woman struggles with the racist atmosphere in her workplace. A bishop devises a novel method to make sure his congregants pass Tithing Settlement. Parents hire men to pose as the Three Nephites to teach their children the Book of Mormon is true. Ex-Mormons unwelcome at home for Christmas band together for their own holiday celebration.

Sex on the Sabbath

A missionary in Italy tries to rescue a woman enslaved in trafficking. A Salt Lake bishop is murdered in his office. A Mormon advice columnist gets into trouble with the Church. Parents arrange to kidnap their missionary son and force him into deprogramming. A disabled woman questions her Patriarchal Blessing's admonition to remain celibate her entire life. A husband chafes when his wife won't let him watch R-rated movies. A desperate man takes horrifying measures to pay his bills. A straight high school senior asks his gay friend to the prom. Even a near-death experience doesn't convince a skeptic of the existence of God. A chaste Single Adult group ventures into the French Quarter on Mardi Gras. God's visit to a fourteen-year-old girl doesn't go as planned. The marriage of a couple who manage to leave the Mormon Church together is newly stressed when one of them becomes a devout member of another organization.

The Tyranny of Silence

An Artificial Intelligence tries to lead Mormons astray. The Church addresses the perils of inappropriate hair styles for men. A bereaved widow listens to the radio hoping to hear love songs from her departed husband. A high school teacher is stalked by one of her students. An obese man struggles to lead a meaningful life. A prankster makes life miserable for his LDS boss. An ex-Mormon earns a living selling Mormon underwear online to non-members. A young man fakes a two-year mission to please his family. Another missionary targets potential converts on dating sites. A lonely husband pays the price for straying from his wife. Joseph Smith takes action when he discovers Emma's polyandrous marriage. The Church reels after a leak that children of gay couples can no longer participate in its saving rituals and ordinances. A depressed Santa reaches out to help his community.

Selling the City of Enoch

In this collection of Mormon short stories, we see a mission president's wife murdered in Rome. A man whose past is filled with abuse learns to love for the first time. A mother plans for her role as a god in the hereafter. A descendant of Enoch tries out capitalism. A husband nearing his seventh wedding anniversary leads a secret life. A bishop disguises himself as a homeless man to teach his congregation a lesson. A lonely young woman rents a mother and father for Christmas. A young husband is horrified to learn he has married a pre-op male-to-female trans woman in the temple. A group of ex-Mormons meet regularly to watch LDS movies in order to keep in touch with their culture.

The Mormon Inquisition

Decades after the Fall, archeologists excavating ruins discover an abandoned vault deep in a mountainside. The vault has been seriously compromised, but a few documents have been found printed on actual paper, an astonishing recovery after worldwide climate disaster has all but wiped out forests. The researchers carefully peruse the documents, a series of stories about everyday Mormons, to learn about the glories of the past. But the disturbing discoveries they make leave them on the verge of forbidding further exploration altogether.

Interview with a Mission President

Jason Kincaid is nearing the end of his three-year term as president of the Washington Seattle mission of the LDS Church. His service has been difficult, and for the first time in his life, he has doubts. During the last zone conference over which he presides, he does something he's never done before. In each of his interviews with the missionaries serving under him, he asks them to openly discuss their own doubts. He hopes that by building up their faith, he will rebuild his own. What happens instead will rock the entire Church to its core.

The Last Days Linger

The scriptures tell us that in the Last Days, wickedness will increase upon the Earth. When leaders of the Mormon Church see a rise in the number of gay members, they believe the end is upon them. But while "wickedness never was happiness," it begins to appear that wickedness can sometimes be divine. At least, the stories here suggest that religious proscriptions condemning homosexuality have it all wrong. While gay Mormons may be no closer to perfection than anyone else, they're no further from it, either. And sometimes, being gay provides just the right ingredient to create saints—as flawed as God himself.

The Moat around Zion

A moat can work to keep bad guys out of one's sanctuary, but it can also act like a prison, trapping good people inside, and the stench from its fetid waters can often prove unbearable. In these tales of the trapped faithful, a woman is shunned when a hacker fakes her apostasy from the Mormon Church. A young missionary can't get permission to see a doctor about the lump on his testicle until he can convince his mission president he isn't masturbating. A lesbian couple wonder if their desperate financial situation is a punishment from God. A disillusioned man tries to train himself to stop praying. A teenage girl impersonates her brother so she can perform baptisms for the dead in the temple. Two gay missionaries in Italy fall in love. The stories in this collection show that while fences may be good at keeping people out who want to come in, they are also quite effective at keeping people in who want to get out.

Mormon Madness

Mental illness can strike the faithful as easily as anyone else. But often religious doctrine and practice exacerbate rather than alleviate these problems. From schizophrenia to obsessive-compulsive disorder, from persecution complex to sexual dysfunction, autism to dissociative identity disorder, Mormons must cope with their mental as well as their spiritual health on a daily basis.

Human Compassion for Beginners

The battle to direct legislation and policy often seems to be a fight between greed and compassion. Emotions run so high that family members stop speaking to one another and long-time friendships fall by the wayside. But the problems being debated—climate change, universal healthcare, LGBTQ rights, gun regulation, economic inequality, and the separation of church and state—desperately need to be resolved.

In this volume, Johnny Townsend, author of *The Tyranny of Silence* and *The Washing of Brains*, shares many of the ideas he's published in *The Salt Lake Tribune*, *LA Progressive*, *Main Street Plaza*, and a variety of other publications on these and many more vital issues of our day.

Dead Mankind Walking

Do you yell at the TV while watching the news? Do you repost maddening articles on Facebook? Do you find yourself overwhelmed by the 200 new political emails in your inbox every day? Left, right, center, far left, or far right, we can't escape the political battles of our time.

What this collection of essays and op-eds from *LA Progressive*, *The Salt Lake Tribune*, and *Main Street Plaza* can do is help us understand and address many of the concerns that affect almost every aspect of our lives: structural racism, gerrymandering, voting rights, regressive taxes, political infighting, the failure of capitalism, and the ever present overstep of religion in public policy.

But of all the issues covered here, the most urgent is climate change. If we can't address that one, the others don't much matter, since every one of us all too soon becomes nothing more than a tiny, inescapable part of *Dead Mankind Walking*.

Who Invited You to the Orgy?

Johnny Townsend, author of award-winning literary fiction, whose op-eds have appeared in major newspapers across the country, gives us his most eclectic collection yet. Stories of trans and gay Mormons balancing their spiritual and temporal lives.

Essays on gun reform, universal healthcare, climate change, and the separation of church and state. Concluding with a handful—and mouthful—of erotic tales based on his experiences in a French Quarter gay bookstore and as a young missionary in Italy. A thought-provoking yet entertaining glimpse into the mind and life of a gay ex-Mormon atheist working to unify the disparate components of our lives.

Breaking the Promise of the Promised Land: How Religious Conservatives Failed America

By aligning themselves over the past 60 years with the most conservative wing of the Republican Party, Mormons became leading contributors to the cultural and moral decay of America. Mormon prophets have long declared that God set America apart for the righteous. It was to be a land of freedom, justice, and peace, a place where the Lamanites could blossom as the rose, a country so righteous that the affairs of the entire world would be conducted here during the Millennium.

But when Mormons tired of being "a peculiar people" and chose to side with the most repressive evangelicals, they chose to make America the land of the imprisoned, poor, and oppressed. While declaring their allegiance to the Prince of Peace, they've chosen to support policies that have kept America at war almost non-stop for the last six decades.

Perhaps rather than continue following old men who tell them what an invisible God wants them to do, they should consider doing what they can see with their own eyes the people all around them need.

CPSIA information can be obtained
at www.ICGtesting.com
Printed in the USA
FSHW010118160919
62043FS

9 781644 389331